Demographics and the Demand
for Higher Education

DEMOGRAPHICS
and
THE DEMAND FOR HIGHER EDUCATION

Nathan D. Grawe

Johns Hopkins University Press
Baltimore

Johns Hopkins University Press
2715 North Charles Street
Baltimore, Maryland 21218-4363
www.press.jhu.edu

Library of Congress Cataloging-in-Publication Data
Names: Grawe, Nathan D., author.
Title: Demographics and the demand for higher education / Nathan D. Grawe.
Description: Baltimore : Johns Hopkins University Press, 2017. | Includes
    bibliographical references and index.
Identifiers: LCCN 2017009943 | ISBN 9781421424132 (hardcover : alk. paper) |
    ISBN 1421424134 (hardcover : alk. paper) | ISBN 9781421424149 (electronic) |
    ISBN 1421424142 (electronic)
Subjects: LCSH: Education, Higher—United States—Forecasting | Education,
    Higher—Economic aspects—United States. | Education—Demographic
    aspects—United States. | Universities and colleges—United States—Administration. |
    Population geography—United States. | United States—Population. | BISAC:
    EDUCATION / Higher. | BUSINESS & ECONOMICS / Economics / General. | SOCIAL
    SCIENCE / Demography. | EDUCATION / Educational Policy & Reform / General.
Classification: LCC LA227.4 .G736 2017 | DDC 378.00973—dc23
    LC record available at https://lccn.loc.gov/2017009943

A catalog record for this book is available from the British Library.

Special discounts are available for bulk purchases of this book.
For more information, please contact Special Sales at 410-516-6936 or
specialsales@press.jhu.edu.

Johns Hopkins University Press uses environmentally friendly book
materials, including recycled text paper that is composed of at least
30 percent post-consumer waste, whenever possible.

To Heather, Hannah, Toby, Caleb, and Noah—
Soli Deo Gloria

Contents

Acknowledgments

This project began with an invitation from Bev Nagel, Carleton College's dean of the college, to serve in her office as associate dean of the college from 2009 through 2012. Her invitation set me off in completely new scholarly directions through the administrative problems encountered while working in that role. Once the work was under way, I received invaluable feedback from Jenny Bourne and participants in the St. Olaf–Carleton seminar on socioeconomic inequality. Expert input was generously provided by colleagues at Carleton and other colleges. Bev, Steve Poskanzer, and Paul Thiboutot (Carleton College) and Scott Bierman and Nancy Benedict (Beloit College) suggested revisions that were critically important to the ultimate form of the forecast model. And Michael Hemesath and Cal Mosley (St. John's University) and Matthew Malatesta (Union College) helped me understand the best way to apply my work to be most useful to admissions officers. Carleton GIS specialist Wei-Hsin Fu led me through the trials of using GIS mapping software; without her help, I would no doubt still be in a basement computer lab. Carleton student Greg Sharpe provided tremendous research assistance by developing the GIS mapping layouts for various figures. Last, but not least, Carleton staff members Paula Lackie, Kim Bradley, Holly Rapp, and Deborah Sunderland supplied essential IT and facilities support.

Social scientists are always dependent on their data. This project is no different. I am incredibly grateful to the US Census Bureau and Department of Education for collecting the information used here. I hope my work is one more piece of evidence in support of efforts to measure the state of our nation. I am further thankful to the National Center for Education Statistics and the Minnesota Population Center for posting the Education Longitudinal Study (ELS) and the American Community Survey online. In the former case, I also thank all of those who are responsible for administering the restricted portion of the dataset so that respondents' privacy is maintained while giving researchers access to invaluable information. Finally, I thank the ELS respondents for their willingness to provide private information over many years. My work would literally be impossible without their cooperation.

Of course, no research project runs on resources from work alone. My parents spent many hours listening to my ideas, sharpening them by asking questions, and providing expert writing advice. My children Hannah, Toby, Caleb, and Noah gave up more than a few summer days and school-year weekends with me so that I could work. Most of all, Heather, my wife, made sure everything continued to run at home. She keeps things on track when I don't, fills in the gaps that I leave behind, and generally holds us all together. This work would simply have been impossible without her many contributions.

Finally, I am grateful for editorial support from Johns Hopkins University Press. Reviewers suggested smart revisions which greatly improved the final result, and Greg Britton and Catherine Goldstead provided steady encouragement and expert advice essential to sharing my ideas with others.

Demographics and the Demand for Higher Education

Introduction

In recent years, pessimistic forecasters have made a cottage industry telling stories of higher education's impending collapse under the weight of looming demographic change. As if it were not enough that demographic trends have steadily nudged the population toward subgroups with weak attachments to higher education, the Great Recession caused birth rates to plummet almost 13 percent in just five years. (Chapters 1 and 2 document the trends most relevant for higher education demand.) In light of these intense pressures, the dominant narrative offers up fear. For example, the lead in the January 24, 2014, *Chronicle of Higher Education* bore the headline "The Class of 2030" in reference to the issue's feature article on the demographic effects on future classes of college entrants. Accompanied by a map showing the number of 4-year-olds relative to 18-year-olds by county (a map dripping with deep-red ink), the article reached a broad and devastating conclusion: "Until just a few years ago, colleges could anticipate classes of high-school graduates each bigger than the last. . . . But those days are over" (A24).

When, as an administrator, I first saw these forecasts, my initial response was something like, "I'd better keep my résumé up to date in case I need to find a different line of work!" But whether through disciplinary training or simple survival instinct, a second thought soon dominated the first: "What, if anything, do these figures say about *my* institution's future?" After all, for better or worse, not all young people are equally likely to attend college, much less college of a particular type or in a particular region. As I looked for better data to help me understand the challenges ahead, the best I could find were forecasts of high school graduates made by the Western Interstate Commission for Higher Education (WICHE). While WICHE's adjustments for high school completion are a step in the right direction, if these are the only data available, then administrators and policymakers alike are heading toward the heart of a demographic tempest without a map or a compass.

This book fills that gap with the Higher Education Demand Index (HEDI). Described in detail in chapter 3 and the methodological appendix, the HEDI uses data from the 2002 Education Longitudinal Study (ELS) to estimate the probability of college-going conditional on basic demographic variables: sex, race/ethnicity, parent education, geographic location, family income, family composition, and nativity. Depending on demographic characteristics, young people experience vastly different likelihoods of college attendance. The extraordinary range in college-going probabilities can be seen by comparing a pair of hypothetical children. The first is a native-born Asian American woman living in Boston with both parents. Each parent acquired education beyond a bachelor's degree, and their family income totals $125,000. The second student is a native-born Hispanic man living in rural California with his single mother, who does not have a high school diploma. Their family income is only $40,000. Based on experiences reported in the ELS, the probability that the former student will attend a four-year college exceeds 95 percent. By contrast, the likelihood of four-year college attendance for the latter student is less than 10 percent. If we instead consider attendance at an institution ranked among the top 50 colleges or universities, the former probability still exceeds 70 percent, while the latter falls to just 2 percent.

When demographic groups differ 10- or 30-fold in the probability of college attendance, it is clear that reliable estimates of the future demand for higher education require more than forecasts of headcounts or even high school graduates. Expected fluctuations in total populations simply do not contain sufficient information, particularly for more selective forms of education, which by definition have low attendance rates. Accounting for differences in the probability of college attendance across demographic groups doesn't simply modify the picture painted by the dominant narrative. Depending on the type of institution considered, it entirely reverses the story line from one of plummeting populations to one of robust growth.

With the HEDI model in hand, chapters 4 through 6 explore anticipated shifts in demand within higher education as a whole and by institution type. Chapters 4 and 5 show that college attendance and attendance at two-year schools look like a slightly exaggerated version of the pessimistic forecasts of population and high school graduates. Adjustments for the probability of college matriculation are simply too small to overcome the forces of demography. By contrast, in chapter 6 we see that demand for four-year schools will outperform population forecasts such that some subportions of higher education can expect booming future demand. Reflecting increasing numbers of Asian Americans and children with BA-holding parents, the model predicts particularly robust growth in the pool of students whose demographic markers suggest that they will attend top-ranked schools. Within this rosy outlook lies an important challenge for elite institutions: the collapse of markets in New England and the eastern half of the Midwest. Even before the effects of the birth dearth are felt, schools drawing students from these regions will need to find new recruitment pools to offset falling prospective student pools.

While colleges clearly worry about shrinking numbers of students, the rapid expansion of high-tuition/high-aid financial models means that the economic health of many institutions increasingly depends on full-pay students. Chapter 7 applies the HEDI to this important subgroup, projecting numbers of students whose family income and parental education suggest an ability and willingness to pay expensive tuition bills. Fortunately for colleges, the trend toward greater higher education among parents suggests growth in this important subpopulation. That said, nearly all of the anticipated growth will be found west of the Mississippi River, with essentially no expansion expected in the traditional northeastern market. Schools in this traditional center of higher education should not expect to be given relief by falling discount rates.

As important as the HEDI forecasts may be, it is even more important for institutions and policymakers to consider how best to react to changes ahead. Drawing on the existing literature, it is possible to identify a wide range of potential responses, including changes to tenure, recruitment strategies, the use of technology in teaching, and public subsidies to increase attendance among groups with lower matriculation rates. Chapter 8 puts the HEDI to use by modeling how future demand might change if recruitment efforts and policy innovations halved gaps in college-going across dimensions of race/ethnicity and income. For two-year and regional four-year institutions, the results are sobering: even under very optimistic assumptions, the number of college students will contract throughout much of the country, including the high-attendance Midwest and Northeast regions. At more selective schools, the picture is more sanguine, though the model still foresees contraction in those traditionally strong markets.

Chapters 9 and 10 continue to study the "what if" analysis, but from the perspective of policymakers. Rather than exploring the composition of the college-going population, these chapters look at how alternations to public policy might affect the rate of attendance with a focus on enrollment gaps across income and race/ethnicity groups. While economic research suggests that efforts to expand access can be effective when properly designed, even aggressive changes will be leaning into a strong demographic headwind. Even halving income and race effects won't substantially reduce current attendance gaps.

The final chapter closes with a look into the 2030s, beyond the model's forecast horizon. While savvy policy should anticipate the changes that demography has already set in motion, the most sophisticated decision makers will go beyond that, considering where trends will head next. While the model's design limits its projections to children who are already born, the lessons from the analysis in preceding chapters point to key trends that will foretell what happens next. Critical among these is the birth rate, which currently sits at historic lows. While the most recent data suggest we may have found a bottom, higher education decision makers can take note of shifts in this key variable to anticipate future reversals in enrollment trends.

In my experience as an administrator, I witnessed firsthand the effects of the Great Recession on college and university decision making. As never before, administrators and trustees understand that major decisions must be grounded in hard data. While doing research for this project, every administrator I spoke with was aware that we are flying blind into a dangerous period for higher education. Yet, just 10 years before the brunt of the current birth dearth is abruptly felt in admissions offices across the country, we still lack demand forecasts that treat selective, national schools as distinct from the local community college. Decisions in the next five years will be critical in determining whether institutions thrive or flounder. By informing those choices with nuanced forecasts, the analysis of this book promises to be an important guide for those responsible for leading institutions of higher education through the storm.

Chapter One

Demographic Headwinds
for Higher Education

E veryone in higher education agrees that dramatic shifts in demand lie ahead, but few seem to understand their situation with the clarity required for decisive action. This is hardly surprising given the contradictory signals: geographic, birth rate, and race/ethnicity trends point toward fewer future college students, while rising parental education suggests movement in the opposite direction. And none of the available forecasts makes an attempt to weight students by their probability of college attendance, much less by their attendance at an institution of any particular type. As any admissions officer can confirm, while the *number* of college-aged children is an important component of higher education demand, *who* is in the prospective student pool is at least as important. With evidence as weak as this, it is understandably difficult to generate buy-in for potentially disruptive policy change. The Higher Education Demand Index, introduced in chapter 3, will remedy this problem with a model that combines a wide range of changing demographic factors, using appropriate weights reflecting probabilities of attendance, into a single measure. Moreover, the HEDI differentiates among different institutional types, separately forecasting demand for two- and four-year colleges or regional, national, and elite colleges and universities.

To be sure, some subsectors of postsecondary education draw such large fractions of the population that no reasonable accounting for the probability of college attendance can offset coming changes in population size and composition. However, subsequent chapters show that, for some institution types, accounting for the probability of college attendance entirely reverses the demographic narrative. Far from being a period of continual retrenchment, the coming decades will bring robust growth. Even within an institution type, expected changes in demand will vary by geographic region. In short, a true telling of the demographic story is complex with both winners and losers.

But before presenting alternative forecasts, this chapter and the next describe major demographic changes that serve as inputs to the model. While some of these are long-standing and will be familiar to readers, the Great Recession created important breaks in trend that may be less well known. A detailed understanding of these underlying forces will be critical to interpreting HEDI projections. This chapter covers the pessimistic signals that have received the greatest attention, while the next presents reasons we might hope the future is not dictated by these simple population movements.

Key Demographic Headwinds

There is no argument: demographic change is reshaping the population of the United States in ways that raise challenges for higher education. Through immigration, interstate migration, and fertility differences across demographic groups, the country's population is tilting toward the Southwest in general and the Hispanic Southwest in particular. From the perspective of the higher education sector, these changes adversely shift the population away from traditionally strong markets toward those with lower rates of educational acquisition. While colleges and universities have the advantage of an 18-year lead time when confronting demographic changes, the trends described in this chapter are large, and postsecondary institutions have not always proven the most agile market participants. Little time remains to determine the meaning of these changes for higher education and to respond accordingly.

As colleges and universities grapple with these existing trends in the marketplace, an emerging demographic phenomenon will make their work much more difficult. In an apparent response to the financial crisis, the nation's total fertility rate has plummeted by more than 12 percent since 2007. And so, beginning in 2026 the number of native-born children reaching college age will begin a rapid decline. The most recent data suggests fertility rates may have reached a bottom in 2013, but nothing so far suggests a meaningful recovery. The Great Recession did not simply delay births—it eliminated them.

IMMIGRATION

For many, immigration is woven into the very identity of America. In part, this reflects the fact that the majority of Americans can trace their family's arrival in North America to a point in the past 200 years. For others, the immigrant identity stems more from the country's collective history welcoming new people into American society. The Department of Homeland Security's *Homeland Security Yearbook of Immigration Statistics: 2015* (table 1) reports the number of people obtaining lawful resident status each year since the turn of the last century. According to the report, between 1900 and 2015 more than 60 million persons gained this status. Following lulls around the First and Second World Wars, the level of legal immigration increased more or less linearly, each decade bringing a larger number of new residents than the decade before. This is true even of the 2000s, despite the enormous spike around 1990 created by amnesty provisions in the 1986 Immigration Reform and Control Act (IRCA). Today, nearly one million people gain lawful resident status each year.

Unauthorized immigration adds to these legal immigrant flows. To put the number of undocumented residents in context, Hoefer and colleagues (2012) estimate 11.5 million unauthorized immigrants lived in the United States as of January 2011. In other words, the current number of undocumented immigrants amounts to roughly 20 percent of the entire legal immigrant population for the past century. Until the recent recession, which cut the rate of undocumented immigration in half, the authors estimate that approximately 600,000 undocumented immigrants were added to this total annually. Given these authorized and unauthorized immigrant totals, the nonnative population has unequivocally altered the current US population in general and the population of those of college-going age in particular.

Of course, the impact of these immigration levels cannot be well understood without placing it in the context of population size. Even as the number of those obtaining lawful permanent resident status has increased decade after decade, the country's population has grown at a pace more or less equal to the rise in immigrants so that the immigration rate has remained relatively stable. During the 1980s, approximately 2.4 new immigrants were admitted residency for every 1,000 US residents. In 1989 the IRCA temporarily tripled the immigration rate as previously undocumented immigrants attained legal status, but by 1992 or 1993 immigration rates fell again to "normal" levels. Since the IRCA, the rate has been somewhat higher than in the 1980s—an average of 3.3 new legal residents per 1,000 US residents. Whether we view this difference as random noise (in the post-IRCA era, immigration rates have varied between 2.4 and 4.2 per 1,000 residents) or as part of a trend, it seems better to view the forces of immigration on future higher education demand like a constant stream rather than a sudden deluge.

International comparison provides a useful point of reference when thinking about the relative importance of American immigration. An Organisation for Economic Co-operation and Development (OECD) study of 26 national censuses taken near the year 2000 finds that the percentage of the US population born elsewhere is very comparable to that of other developed countries (Dumont and Lemaître 2005). At 12.3 percent, the United States ranks eighth—only slightly higher than the median and almost exactly at the average within the group. Several other countries clearly surpass the United States in this measure: Luxembourg's share of nonnative residents exceeds 30 percent, while approximately 20 percent of those living in Australia, Switzerland, New Zealand, and Canada were born elsewhere. Based on this measure alone, one might question the title of John F. Kennedy's famous *A Nation of Immigrants.*

While the *rate* of immigration in the United States does not stand out from that of OECD peers, the *nature* of US immigration is exceptional in the degree to which immigrants are drawn from poorer parts of the world. This is immediately evident when examining the share of foreign-born residents originating from Europe and North America. While 80 percent of the US foreign-born hail from other parts of the world, in many European countries non-Euro/American immigrants account for less than 10 percent of the foreign-born population (Dumont and Lemaître 2005).[1] On average, OECD countries draw only 20 percent of foreigners from outside these affluent Western centers. Only Japan exceeds the United States in taking in immigrants from other parts of the world—perhaps an unremarkable achievement given its location in Asia. Apparently, free movement within the European Union results in large foreign-born populations, but the foreign-born look remarkably like natives in an economic sense. A heavy draw from developing nations continues to be an important feature of US immigration: from 2004 to 2013, between 38 and 40 percent of newly legalized US permanent residents originated from Asia and South or Central America, respectively (Department of Homeland Security 2014, table 3).

In addition to directly altering the racial/ethnic distribution of the US population, immigrant flows also indirectly affect future demand for higher education via effects on the geographic distribution. Lumpiness of the immigrant population across states stems from several possibly interacting causes. First, a small number of cities serve as disembarkation points. For example, for the decade ending in 2015, the 39 states with the fewest numbers of new permanent residents together accounted for fewer new legal residents than the single state of California, which alone claimed more than 215,000 per year (Department of Homeland Security 2016, table 4). Florida and New York–New Jersey reported about 120,000 and 200,000 new legal residents per year, respectively, over the same period. Texas rounded out the most popular disembarkation points with not quite 100,000 new legal residents per year. While permanent residents subsequently spread throughout the country (see the methodological appendix for more on this), their impact is disproportionately felt in the Southwest and along the Atlantic coast. Research suggests that states that become homes to a critical mass of immigrants may attract even more immigrants as new arrivals seek out neighborhoods and cities where their home culture is present. Economists further argue that immigrant-friendly public policies (which might be influenced by large immigrant populations) serve as "immigrant magnets," drawing populations to some states and cities more than others (Bartel 1989, Borjas 1999, Brücker et al. 2002, De Giorgi and Pellizzari 2009, and Razin and Wahba 2015).

Taken together, the large and increasing flow of immigrants from Asia and Central and South America has and will continue to shift the US population toward greater shares among Hispanic, Asian, and Southwest subgroups. Because immigration rates have been more or less steady over the past three decades, we should expect consistent pressures in these directions. If policymakers implement a new immigration reform akin to the IRCA or if a version of the Development, Relief, and Education for Alien Minors (DREAM) Act is passed, we would expect demand for higher education to shift even further in these directions.

INTERSTATE MIGRATION

Just as immigrants cross international borders, existing residents move between states and cities within the country, affecting future markets for higher education. Figure 1.1 maps net migration rates among children as reported in 2011, the most recent year available in the American Community Survey.[2] Even in this single year, we see clear evidence of interstate migration of children out of the Northeast and into the South and West. Some of the observed rates of change are quite dramatic. For example, in just one year New York City netted a loss of 0.6 percent, while Charlotte gained 0.9 percent. Of course, not all migration is equally disruptive to the future of higher education. For example, if the negative

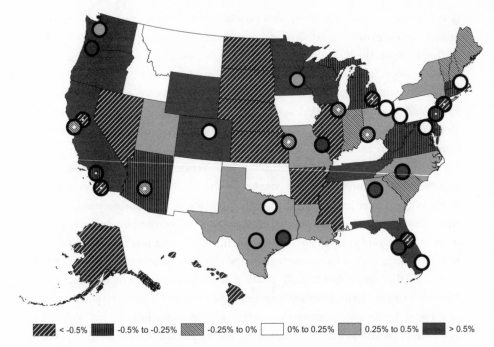

Figure 1.1. Net migration rate between cities and nonmetropolitan portions of states for children ages 2 to 17 between the years 2010 and 2011. *Note:* The net migration rate is the difference between in-migration and out-migration divided by the 2010 population of children ages 2 to 17. *Source:* Author's calculations based on 2011 American Community Survey

and positive net migration rates in Orlando and Tampa simply represented movements from the former to the latter, then many colleges and universities may experience little pressure to dramatically change recruitment strategies. For this reason, it may be helpful to consider migration on the level of the nine census divisions. While obscuring important intradivisional differences, this aggregation makes clearer the broad pattern of net flows from the Pacific and Middle Atlantic to the West South Central. All other divisions have experienced more or less offsetting out- and in-migration as net growth in one state or city is balanced against losses seen in a nearby state or city.

While migration patterns in 2010 in part reflect responses to the financial crisis and subsequent recession, a Pew Research Center study confirms that the general patterns mentioned previously are consistent with trends evident in US Census data from 1975 to 2007.[3] Like immigration, it would appear that the migratory forces nudging the population away from the Northeast and Pacific toward the South are persistent, and we should expect the trend to continue.

Birth Rates across Race/Ethnicity

Even when families do not move across state or international borders, differing birth rates between groups cause changes to demographic distributions. The Centers for Disease Control and Prevention's (CDC) *National Vital Statistics Reports* note marked differences in total fertility rates by race/ethnicity (CDC 2017, table 8).[4] Over the past 25 years, the total fertility rate among both Hispanic and non-Hispanic black women has exceeded the national average. Fertility among the latter, which stood 20 percent above average in the early 1990s, has reverted to the mean, such that total fertility in this group in 2015 fell within a percent of the national benchmark. Though total fertility among Hispanic women has also trended toward the mean, it remains much higher than average even today. From 1990 through the mid-2000s, the excess in Hispanic fertility relative to the national mean slowly drifted from 40 percent down to around 35 percent. The Great Recession created noticeably greater downward pressure, and in 2015 the total fertility rate among Hispanic women rests only 15 percent higher than the national average. Higher fertility rates among Hispanic and non-Hispanic black women have been balanced by those of non-Hispanic white women. Fertility rates in this subgroup have run 5 to 10 percent below the national average. In total, while fertility gaps between groups have narrowed substantially (particularly since the onset of the financial crisis), the total fertility rate among Hispanic women remains nearly 25 percent higher than that for non-Hispanic whites.

These variations across race/ethnicity amplify regional differences, creating substantial variation across the states. Figure 1.2 maps recent total fertility rates by state. In patterns that echo those found in migration, fertility rates in the Northeast are particularly low, while more births are found west of the Mississippi. Given the strong Northeastern bent of higher education demand, the regional differences seen in figure 1.2 are potentially worrisome. Even ignoring these differences across regions, the fertility level raises concerns for an industry that has come to count on constant or increasing numbers of students. To maintain a stable population over time without immigration, a society must average a bit more than two children per woman—one to replace the woman, one for a male mate, and a bit more to account for child mortality. Only the states colored in black in figure 1.2—eight in total—reach this mark. Moreover, while higher

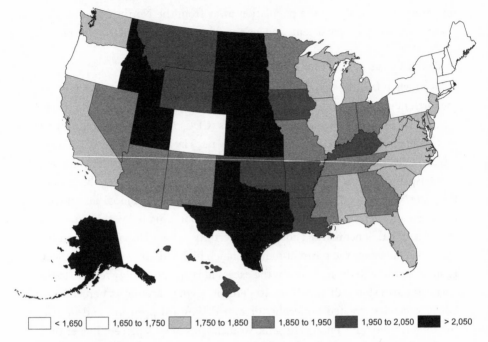

Figure 1.2. Total fertility rate per 1,000 women by state, 2015. *Source:* National Vital Statistics Reports 66 (1): table 12

education institutions of all types have disproportionately relied on students from the Northeast, no state from New York to Maine has a total fertility rate higher than the replacement rate. The most fertile of these falls more than 15 percent below the replacement rate. The number of children being born in this region is simply too small to maintain the population without large infusions from other areas. While the number of immigrants attaining legal status in the Northeast is larger than the net out-migration of that region, the number of immigrant children is nowhere near large enough to offset the low fertility rate.

THE SECOND BIRTH DEARTH

The three demographic forces described previously have been persistently, if slowly, reshaping the US population over decades. While these changes can present challenges to higher education as the student body slowly evolves, the pace of change is relatively modest, allowing for incremental, adaptive responses. More recently, we have witnessed an acute change in birth rates that will require changes that are far from incremental. As can be seen in figure 1.3, 2007 marked

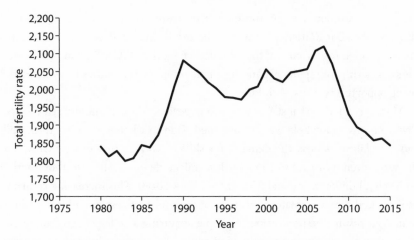

Figure 1.3. Total fertility rate per 1,000 women, 1980 to 2015. *Source:* National Vital Statistics Reports 66 (1): table 4

the beginning of a precipitous reduction in the total fertility rate, which fell more than 12 percent in only six years. After a modest 0.3 percent increase in 2014, the 2015 data show a 1 percent drop, suggesting that we have yet to find the bottom. Fertility rates have not fallen this abruptly since the 1970s. While the effects of immigration and migration will be more evident on campuses over the next decade, beginning in 2026 the birth dearth will command attention.

To put the present fertility reduction in context, from 1960 to 1973 the total fertility rate was cut almost in half (Schoen 2004). Nevertheless, several differences between the current episode and that of the sexual revolution make the recent reduction notable. First, fertility in the 1950s and 1960s—the reference point for the 1970s birth dearth—reflect the exceptional, postwar baby boom. During the boom, fertility rates were approximately one-third higher than in the interwar period. The drop in fertility from the late 1950s through 1965—roughly half of the midcentury dearth—simply represented a reversion to preboom rates as births delayed by war played out. Setting aside the unwinding of the baby boom, the recent fertility reduction is quite similar in magnitude to that of the late 1960s and early 1970s. So, while not unprecedented, the present birth dearth is large and will place higher education under significant strain when young cohorts reach age 18.

There is a second reason to view the current reduction in fertility as notable: the decreasing fertility rate in the middle of the twentieth century coincided with economic transformation. From 1948 to 1980, the labor force participation rate among women ages 16 and older rose from 33.9 percent to 51.5 percent (Bureau of Labor Statistics 2014). At the same time, college graduation rates among women rose from half that of men to near parity (Goldin and Katz 2006). This was a time of rapidly expanding employment opportunities for women and rising opportunity costs of children.

Moreover, it wasn't just women who experienced an economic sea change. The economy as a whole was transformed. Due to what economists term *skill-biased technical change*, the demand for skilled workers rose dramatically, and the wage premium paid to those with a college degree relative to those with a high school diploma doubled (Goldin and Katz 2008). This increasing return to skill created a much greater incentive for parents to invest in children's education. As a result, the proportion of people acquiring a college degree increased approximately 150 percent from 1950 to 1980. This trend cushioned the demand reduction that would have otherwise followed from low birth rates. Economic theorists such as Gary Becker (1981) explained that the increasing demand for education created a simultaneous reduction in fertility, as larger educational investments represented a significant increase in the cost of offspring. Given changing sex roles and returns to skill during that time period, it is perhaps unsurprising that fertility shifted so dramatically in the 1960s and 1970s. Without similarly transformative economic trends, the size of the current fertility reduction appears quite large.

The most commonly cited cause of the present birth dearth is delayed fertility driven by economic uncertainty among those in childbearing ages. (See Cherlin et al. 2013, Goldstein et al. 2013, and Sobotka et al. 2011 for studies of the Great Recession and fertility in the United States and Europe.) Consistent with this explanation, from the start of the crisis birth rates have fallen for every age group younger than 29 years and have increased for every age group older than 30 years (CDC 2016). While trends toward childbearing later in life began in the early 1990s, the rates of change were amplified following the financial crisis. This interpretation leaves open the possibility that, like the baby boom following World War II, many of the "missing" children of the financial crisis may reappear following a full economic recovery. However, given the biology of fecundity, every year that passes makes it less and less likely that young families today will achieve the same ultimate family size that they would have absent the present reduction in fertility. Either way, beginning in the mid-2020s many colleges will enter an extended period of shrinking recruitment pools.

Predicted Changes to the Number of High School Graduates

These demographic trends and others play out in forecasts of future high school graduates published by the Western Interstate Commission for Higher Education (WICHE).[5] In aggregate, the WICHE prediction plotted in figure 1.4 provides reason for medium-term optimism, as it signals a healthy 5 percent rise in the number of public and private high school graduates over the next decade. While approximately one-half of this gain represents a recovery from a recent decrease in high school graduates, WICHE expects the number of diploma-holders to reach new highs in the mid-2020s. Following this run-up, the aftershocks of the birth dearth will create a sharp, 9 percent pullback. In aggregate, the number of high school graduates in the late 2020s may not differ much from today, but the uneven path to that point suggests potential challenges to institutional planning.

Aggregate forecasts conceal geographic variations that further complicate the future for higher education. When WICHE predictions are broken down by census division, the results clearly illustrate the cumulative effects of the demographic forces discussed earlier. (Graphs of regional forecasts are available with supplemental materials on the book's website.[6]) The number of high school graduates in New England and the East North Central are expected to fall by 15 to 20 percent. Unfortunately, these areas of greatest loss are among the strongest

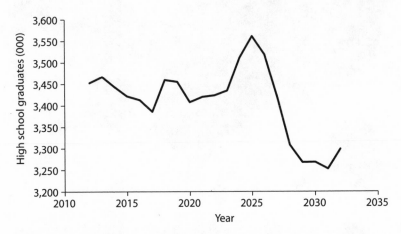

Figure 1.4. Forecasted number of high school graduates by year of high school graduation, 2012 to 2032. *Source:* Western Interstate Commission for Higher Education (2016)

prospective student pools for higher education. What is more, the aggregate growth in high school graduates expected through 2025 is supported almost entirely by increases in the Mountain and West South Central divisions—regions that have historically had modest connections to higher education systems.

Examining the same data at the state level shows that the changes seen at the divisional level are experienced by most states within a division, with very few exceptions. Figure 1.5 maps the results. For example, the number of high school graduates is expected to fall by at least 20 percent in each state in New England with the exception of Massachusetts, which expects to be down 11 percent. While the forecasts for the East North Central and Middle Atlantic states are somewhat less negative, each and every state in these regions is expected to produce fewer graduates in 2032 than in 2012. This spatial correlation in growth rates of high school graduates potentially augments future recruitment challenges because it will often be impossible to find more promising markets next door to shrinking ones.

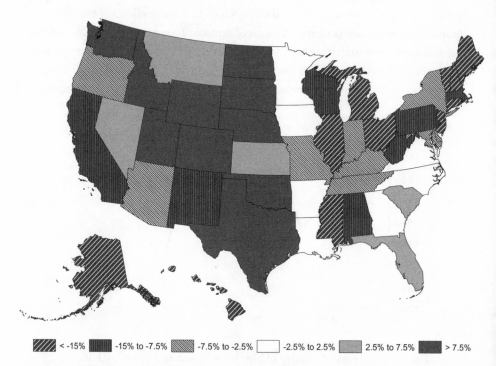

Figure 1.5. Forecasted growth in high school graduates, 2012 to 2032. *Source:* Author's calculations based on Western Interstate Commission for Higher Education (2016)

Because areas differ in population, it is also helpful to look at forecasted changes in absolute terms. With the exception of the West South Central, which is forecast to produce around 70,000 more high school graduates in 2032 than in 2012, the absolute increases in the Mountain, West North Central, and South Atlantic are modest—between 5,000 and 12,000. By contrast, during the same time period the Pacific, Middle Atlantic, and New England divisions will lose between 54,000 and 32,000 students each, while the East North Central falls by more than 90,000. A similar pattern emerges when comparing states of largest increase and decrease: whether looked at on a regional or state level, anticipated losses exceed gains by a two-to-one margin.

If the geographic patterns in high school graduation were not unnerving enough for admissions officers, analyzing the WICHE data by race/ethnicity points to additional challenges. Projections for the number of non-Hispanic white public high school graduates—the largest source of current college students—predict steady decay.[7] Between now and the early 2030s, this group is expected to generate fewer and fewer high school graduates, a decline that is as consistent as it is sharp. Over the horizon of WICHE's forecasts, they anticipate 265,000 fewer high school graduates from this subgroup. While the birth dearth may increase the pace of decline slightly, there is no period of respite before contraction. In total, by 2032 WICHE foresees 15 percent fewer non-Hispanic white high school graduates than there are today.

Of course, if over the next decade the total number of graduates holds steady or increases while the number of non-Hispanic white graduates steadily declines, this means that high school graduates of minority race/ethnicity must be increasing. Indeed, only the extraordinary effects of the present birth dearth promise to slow the rapid rise in minority high school graduates (up one-fifth by 2025). Despite the anticipated reversal after 2025, the predicted number of such students increases by more than 15 percent between now and 2032. The number of Asian and Pacific Islander high school graduates is forecast to increase by an even more impressive 35 percent, though from a smaller base number. By contrast, non-Hispanic black graduates are anticipated to fall by 8 percent.

These shifts in race/ethnicity will be experienced broadly throughout the country. Figure 1.6 maps WICHE forecasts of high school graduates for each state by race/ethnicity. That agency expects that the number of Hispanic and Asian and Pacific Islander high school diploma-holders will increase by more than 15 percent in nearly every state. The exceptions are found in the far West and Southwest, where large numbers of these groups already live, making double-digit

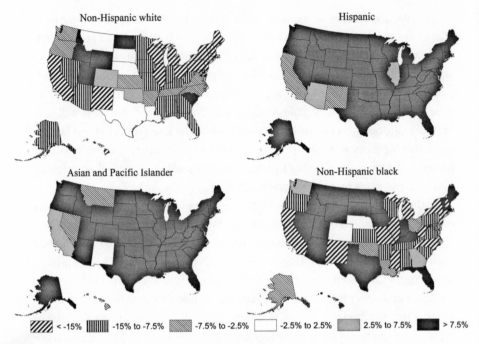

Figure 1.6. Forecasted growth in public high school graduates by race/ethnicity, 2012 to 2032. *Source:* Author's calculations based on Western Interstate Commission for Higher Education (2016)

growth rates difficult to achieve. The expected decline in non-Hispanic white graduates is only slightly less uniform, with small pockets of growth in South Carolina and the Mountain West and deeper than average reductions in the Midwest, Northeast, and Pacific.

A Reason to Pause before Action

In sum, over the next 15 years persistent trends in immigration, migration, and differential birth rates coupled with the recent acute birth dearth will markedly alter the college-aged population along dimensions of geography and race/ethnicity. Non-Hispanic white students from the Midwest and Northeast in particular—groups with the greatest current propensity to attend college—will become far less numerous. In the context of predictions for such rapid change, it is little wonder that organizations such as the College Board have convened conferences designed to encourage institutions to consider significant alterations to recruitment and educational strategies. In addition to shifting recruitment toward higher-growth regions and contemplating changes to application materials and processes, the College Board (2005, 8) suggests that institutions may need to change curricula, alter pedagogy, and provide new support services. Considering the WICHE data, one could argue that the board's list of recommended actions is far too conservative. Total numbers of students are headed toward a cliff. And given forecast patterns across race/ethnicity and geography, the coming contraction in higher education may be proportionately larger than that in high school graduates. Perhaps, institutions need to prepare for significant staff and faculty reductions within the next 15 years and not simply redesign our recruitment and teaching strategies.

Before making sweeping (and sometimes irreversible) changes, it would be wise for institutions to step back for a moment to ask whether the demographic data presented in this chapter necessarily prophesy difficult times that demand radical action. There are two arguments in the negative. First, the data mentioned above show significant variation across regions. For institutions in high-growth areas, perhaps nothing must be done. "Easy" solutions of this type should be considered with skepticism. In particular, locations of institutions are strongly correlated with locations of current students. So, while there are indeed some institutions well located to benefit from demographic change, many more are situated in areas of loss. Moreover, the logic of this counterargument ignores likely changes in other institutions' behaviors. In response to shrinking student pools, we should expect institutions in declining markets to alter recruitment strategies, expanding into high-growth areas. This will create greater competition for institutions already located in those areas. Given that the aggregate trend is negative, increased competition could easily outstrip expected growth, leaving fewer students even for institutions located in areas expecting healthy growth in the number of young people.

There is a second and better reason to reserve judgment based on the headcount data alone. It ignores information critical to understanding the demand for higher education: the probability of college attendance in general and at an institution of a given type in particular. If the size of a recruitment pool is less important than who is in that pool, forecasted changes in the total college-aged population (or even high school graduates) are poor proxies for college demand. Analyzing subsets of the population according to geography or race/ethnicity represents a step in the right direction, in that college-going differs markedly across these subgroups. But even within these groups, the probability of attending college (much less attending a four-year college or an elite four-year college) varies substantially. For example, it is clear that fertility has dropped precipitously in the Northeast. But who accounts for this change? Are high-education, high-income families having fewer children, or are lower-income families reducing family size to cope with the consequences of the Great Recession? The former would be worrisome for elite institutions, while the latter has implications for two-year schools. Clearly, actionable forecasts of future demand must differentiate between submarkets within higher education and explicitly account for the probability of college attendance. Chapter 2 surveys what we know about college-going probabilities and, specifically, connections to trending demographic variables. As we make this step away from simple headcounts and toward a probability-weighted model of higher education demand, we will see that not all of the current demographic trends suggest a dark future for colleges and universities.

Chapter Two

Demographics as Destiny?

The demographic trends and forecasts presented in chapter 1 are surely sobering to many higher education leaders. Clearly, we must anticipate shifts in the college-aged population away from geographic and race/ethnicity subgroups that are well connected with higher education and toward those that have low postsecondary schooling attendance rates. Many have looked at these population forecasts and have drawn the conclusion of a January 24, 2014, *Chronicle of Higher Education* cover story: "Colleges, Here is Your Future." Or, as McGee puts it, "Bienvenido al Futuro de los Estados Unidos" (2016, 37). The Higher Education Demand Index, introduced in chapter 3, certainly captures these population changes, but it does so in the context of offsetting trends and varying college attendance probabilities explained in this chapter.

While the broad population forecasts of chapter 1 will clearly affect future higher education demand, it is equally obvious that the demand for higher education does not follow population trends in lockstep. To see this and many observations that follow, it is helpful to consider data on a regional level. The analysis here and in later chapters follows geographic partitions defined by the US Census Bureau, which divides the country into four "regions": West, Midwest, Northeast, and South. Regions are further divided into a total of nine "divisions." The West is broken into the Pacific and Mountain divisions, the Midwest into West and East North Central, the Northeast into the Middle Atlantic and New England, and the South into West and East South Central plus the South Atlantic.

While these regions and divisions were not defined in regard to patterns in college attendance, adhering to them promotes cross comparison with trends reported in other sources.

The disconnection between population and college attendance is immediately evident when comparing attendance rates across census divisions. Figure 2.1 presents attendance rates for four different institution types by division. While the share of children who attend a postsecondary institution of any kind varies only modestly across the country, uptake of more selective forms of higher education differs substantially. For example, children from the Northeast divisions are 40 percent more likely to attend a four-year institution than those from the West and South Central divisions (52 percent for the former as compared to 36 percent for the latter). These geographical differences become even more pronounced (in relative terms) at highly ranked institutions. For example, a child from New England is more than 10 times as likely as a child from the West South Central to attend an institution ranked among either the top 50 colleges or the top 50 universities by *US News & World Report*.

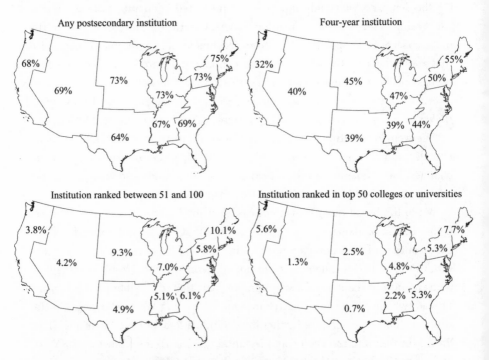

Figure 2.1. College attendance rates by census division. *Source:* Author's calculations based on the 2002 Education Longitudinal Study restricted data

On the surface, these patterns in college attendance seem only to amplify the concerns raised in chapter 1, by quantifying the degree to which the coming population shifts move toward regions with weak attachment to higher education. However, the regional attendance statistics also underscore the important fact that simple headcounts ignore critical differences in college attendance rates that are essential to reliable demand forecasts.[1] Even within a given state or division, children with different family backgrounds and demographic characteristics do not enter equally into the demand function for higher education. Thus changes in the aggregate numbers of children in the nation, a region, or a state need not correspond to proportionate movements in the demand for postsecondary education. It is even quite possible for demand for some subsectors of higher education to grow rapidly despite falling headcounts. Enrollment managers don't need to forecast the number of college-aged children so much as college-bound or two-year college-bound or elite four-year college-bound students (as the case may be). To forecast the degree to which the demographic trends outlined in chapter 1 will affect higher education demand, it is critical to know exactly which families are moving between states, having fewer children, and so forth. Changes among groups with little likelihood of attending a college or university simply won't cause noticeable changes to higher education demand (though we may seek to change these patterns in the future!).

To understand the significance of this point, it is helpful to consider several underlying factors that explain why college-going rates differ so markedly across regions: family income, race/ethnicity, and parent education. In particular, census divisions with strong college uptake also (predictably) tend to have larger proportions of non-Hispanic whites, high-income families, and well-educated parents. Looking at divisions with the most extreme college attendance rates, the demographic differences are stark. For example, the proportion of New England and Middle Atlantic families in the 2002 Education Longitudinal Study (ELS) who reported incomes greater than $100,000 was nearly twice that found in the West South Central. At the other end of the income distribution, only 41 percent and 48 percent of New England and Middle Atlantic families, respectively, reported earnings less than $50,000, as compared with more than 60 percent in the West and East South Central. These income differences are undoubtedly related to differences in the distributions of education and race/ethnicity. In New England, 80 percent of ELS respondents are non-Hispanic whites as compared to 48 percent in the West South Central and 39 percent in the Pacific. The lower numbers of non-Hispanic whites in the latter divisions are explained largely by

Hispanic shares that are three or four times those in New England. Similarly, parents holding advanced degrees are relatively common in New England, where 20 percent of ELS students reported at least one parent with a degree beyond a bachelor's—a status still rare in the West South Central, where only 12 percent of students reported the same. Given these large demographic differences across the divisions, it is little wonder attendance rates are as lumpy as depicted in figure 2.1.

These correlations between demographic characteristics and educational attainment seen at the divisional level are also found at the individual level in the ELS data. Not surprisingly, children from high-income families are much more likely to attend college.[2] When compared with children in families earning less than $50,000 per year in 2002 (the bottom 54 percent of families), children in families with income above $100,000 (i.e., the top 13 percent) are 50 percent more likely to attend a postsecondary institution of some type—a 90 percent attendance rate for the latter as compared to 60 percent for the former. The attendance rate for children from families earning between $50,000 and $100,000 lies almost halfway between these two extremes. Rates of attendance at four-year institutions are similarly correlated with income, with high-income children enjoying a 43-point advantage over their low-income peers (73 percent versus 30 percent, respectively). This difference becomes even sharper at more selective institutions: children from high-income families are more than six times as likely to attend an institution ranked among the top 50 colleges or universities (13 percent as compared to 2 percent).

The correlation between race/ethnicity and college attendance is similarly strong. Asian Americans and non-Hispanic whites are substantially more likely than non-Hispanic blacks and Hispanics to acquire some college education: 84 percent of Asian Americans and 75 percent of non-Hispanic whites attend some postsecondary institution as compared to approximately 60 percent of children in other groups. Again, the differences between demographic groups are more evident at four-year institutions in general and selective four-year institutions in particular. For example, almost half of non-Hispanic whites matriculate to a four-year school, and 5 percent attend a top-50 institution. Asian Americans manage even stronger attendance rates: 58 percent and 15 percent at four-year and elite four-year institutions, respectively. By contrast, only 25 percent of Hispanic students attend any four-year college or university, and just 2 percent go to an institution ranked among the top 50 colleges or universities. (When compared with Hispanics, non-Hispanic blacks are somewhat more likely to attend a four-year institution and somewhat less likely to attend an elite school.)

Finally, educational choices are strongly correlated with parental education. Consider two children. The first has no parental model for completion of high school, while the second lives with at least one parent who possesses a degree beyond a bachelor's. The latter is almost twice as likely as the former (87 percent versus 46 percent) to acquire some postsecondary education. If we set the achievement bar a little higher and ask whether the children attend a four-year institution, the gap is even greater in both absolute and relative terms: 71 percent as compared to 15 percent. In the most extreme comparison, the child of a college degree–holder is more than 12 times as likely to attend a top-ranked institution. Between these extremes, attendance rates consistently grow as this measure of parental education rises from no degree, to a high school diploma, to some college, to a bachelor's degree, to an advanced degree.

A hypothetical example in the introduction showed that demographic characteristics can predict probabilities of college attendance that differ 10- or 30-fold. While the example was chosen to make the point, chapter 3 shows that the conclusion was hardly unique to that particular case. Adjusting for the probability of attendance is much more than a simple accounting exercise. For some regions and subsectors of higher education, the resulting refinements in HEDI forecasts suggest a thriving market despite population losses. In yet more cases, the story is predictably nuanced, with one portion of an institution's market growing and another shrinking.

One key factor in this revised view is the previously noted correlation between parent education and college attendance. Rising educational attainment in the recent past means greater parental educational attainment in the present and future, which, in turn, will likely increase college-going probabilities over time. According to the General Social Survey (Smith et al. 2015), the share of young adults between the ages of 25 and 29 who report that at least one parent holds a bachelor's degree has steadily increased over the past 40 years. In the 1970s, fewer than 15 percent of young adults reported having a bachelor's-holding parent. Through the 1980s and 1990s, that figure consistently increased to almost one-third by 2004, where it remained steady through 2014.

Observations in the 2011 American Community Survey suggest a continuation of this positive trend, which will leave fewer and fewer young people without a family connection to higher education. In that survey, the share of individuals in their 30s holding a bachelor's degree is about 15 percent higher than that observed among individuals in their mid-50s. This change is accounted for by a proportionate reduction in the share of people who hold only a high school diploma. People in their mid-50s represent a large share of the parents of college-aged children today, while those in their 30s will become parents of college-aged children 15 to 20 years from now. So, as educational attainment rises across current adult cohorts, we can expect that future cohorts of 18-year-olds will have parents with higher educational attainment. This fact creates a strong, positive counterforce to the demographic changes noted in chapter 1.

Of course, no accounting for college-going probabilities can entirely negate the power of those aggregate population changes. For example, because the higher education sector as a whole engages roughly 70 percent of young people, when we look at very broad definitions of the higher education market, the positive effects of greater parental education are overwhelmed by the pressures of immigration, migration, and the birth dearth. In this case, there is simply too little difference between "the population as a whole" and "the subset of the population that attends some form of college" for rising parental education to offset a 12-plus percent reduction in the total fertility rate.

However, for subsectors of the industry such as two-year institutions or elite national institutions ranked among the top 50 colleges or universities, it is quite possible for changes in demand to differ markedly from changes in population. Moreover, the massive geographic differences in college attendance rates shown in this chapter mean that the potential space between population and higher education demand will vary substantially by location. To address these complications, the next chapter builds a model of higher education demand that weights population trends according to demographic subgroups' propensity to attend college. The resulting HEDI provides a firmer foundation for higher education planning. After developing the model in chapter 3, the remaining chapters reconsider the narratives laid out in chapter 1 from the perspectives of various institution types and policymakers.

Chapter Three

The Higher Education Demand Index

G rounded in an understanding of major demographic trends that inform the model, this chapter presents a conceptual overview of the Higher Education Demand Index. (For a detailed discussion of variable definitions and methods, consult the methodological appendix.) First, the model is explained and key assumptions are explored. Then, using data from the 2000 Census, the model is tested by comparing its predictions to the populations and college attendance levels actually observed at the national and state/city level over the subsequent dozen years. Despite major disruptions caused by the Great Recession at the end of the 2010s, the model proves to be effective in predicting future college-going behavior.

An Overview of the Higher Education Demand Index

To forecast higher education demand in cities and states over the next 15 to 20 years, we require two pieces of information: (1) how many 18-year-olds there will be in each location and year and (2) what fraction of those children are likely to attend a college or university of a given type. Multiplying the number of children by the probability of attendance yields an expected demand for college:

$$Demand\ for\ College_{lt} = Probability\ of\ Attendance \times Number\ of\ Children_{lt} \equiv PN_{lt} \quad (1)$$

where l represents location and t identifies birth cohorts by the year of expected high school graduation.

As the previous chapter shows, the probability of college-going varies dramatically by location and demographic characteristics. What is more, we may be interested in the higher education demand of various subgroups. For these reasons, we need to allow the probability of college attendance to vary across locations and groups. Suppose there are k different demographic types in each location. For each different demographic type, we can compute an expected number of college-going students using a formula akin to equation 1. Then, to find the total expected demand in location l, we simply add up the number of expected college-going children in each subgroup:

$$Demand\ for\ College_{lt} = P_{l1}N_{l1t} + P_{l2}N_{l2t} + P_{l3}N_{l3t} + \ldots P_{lk}N_{lkt}. \tag{2}$$

The HEDI completes this kind of calculation for each of 63 locations. For the sake of tractability and to reduce problems associated with small subsamples, locations are defined by metropolitan areas and nonmetropolitan portions of states with populations of at least two million people. Because some nonmetropolitan portions of states fall short of this threshold, contiguous states within census divisions are combined when necessary to form areas with populations that meet this threshold.[1] These rules result in a set of locations covering the 28 largest metropolitan areas and 35 nonmetropolitan portions of a state or states. While most later chapters generally present results for these 63 locations, when studying subgroups of the population small sample sizes sometimes require that the analysis be restricted to the level of census division or region.

When interpreting these forecasts, it is important to remember that the model only predicts the number of children who have demographic characteristics recently associated with college attendance. This is not the same as predicting the number of children who will actually attend, because admissions officers may make different choices in the future (and indeed it would be reasonable to expect them to do so given the coming population shifts). The degree to which institutions are able to change admission criteria undoubtedly differs by institution type. Admission standards may be particularly fluid among highly ranked institutions, which have low acceptance rates. Admissions departments at these colleges and universities may raise or lower the bar as necessary to achieve a targeted class size. Thus the forecasts might be better thought of as measures of potential, rather than actual, demand.

While the basic ideas behind equation 2 are straightforward, implementation details introduce more than one complication. The sections that follow outline necessary adjustments to data from the restricted portion of the 2002 Education

Longitudinal Study (ELS) and the 2011 American Community Survey (ACS). After the model is unpacked, the discussion underscores key assumptions underlying the HEDI forecasts. The chapter concludes with a test of the model, using census data from the year 2000 to create population and college matriculation predictions that can be compared with actual observations in the ACS and the 2013 *Digest of Education Statistics*, published by the National Center for Education Statistics (NCES).

Estimating the Probability of College-Going

The HEDI's estimates of college-going probabilities are formed using the ELS, a nationally representative sample of high school sophomores initiated in the year 2002. In its inaugural year, the survey recorded information on basic demographic characteristics, location, and family background for 16,197 students from 750 high schools. A 2006 follow-up survey collected data on 14,011 of the original students, including information on postsecondary schooling. The restricted portion of the survey includes highly detailed observations, including specific postsecondary institutions attended and dates of attendance. Institutions fall into two broad groups—"four-year college or university" and "others"—as categorized by the Integrated Postsecondary Education Data System. In addition, I further subdivide institutions using rankings of *US News & World Report's* national four-year colleges or universities.[2] Using ELS observations, students were coded according to whether they had attended any of the following types of colleges and universities: any postsecondary institution, a two-year college, any four-year college or university, a college or university ranked outside the top 100, a college or university ranked between 51 and 100, and a college or university ranked among the top 50.[3] For ease of reference, top-50 and top-100 institutions will be termed *elite* and *national* schools, respectively, while other four-year institutions are referred to as *regional* institutions.

For each measure of college-going, the HEDI predicts the probability of attendance using a logistic regression with the following explanatory variables: sex, race/ethnicity, an interaction between sex and race/ethnicity, census division and urban/nonurban location of high school, parents' education levels, and family income. Separate regressions are estimated for native-born students living in each of four family composition types (living with both parents, living with mother only, living with father only, and living with neither parent) and for foreign-born students. While the ELS has many additional variables that would clearly improve predictions of college attendance (grade reports, test scores, etc.), the variables in the probability model are intentionally limited to those shared in common by the ELS and the ACS, the source of data for counts of children.

The introduction provided one sharp example of how the probability of college-going can vary dramatically between individual students. Of course, the hypothetical example was not chosen at random. However, figure 3.1, which plots distributions of college-going probabilities estimated for 17-year-olds in the ACS, shows clearly that the message of the hypothetical example reflects a broader reality: young people differ widely in their likelihood of college attendance.[4] (The subsample of 17-year-olds was selected for this figure to mitigate complications related to migration, immigration, and family structure changes—each of which could change between the point of observation in the ACS and college-going if younger children are included.) The top panel presents the distribution of college-going attendance rates for any postsecondary, two-year, and four-year institutions, while the bottom panel focuses on three subgroups of four-year schools. Not surprisingly, the attendance probability distributions shift to the left as more-selective types of institutions are considered. For example, while the median probability of general postsecondary attendance lies near 65 percent, the median for four-year college attendance is only 35 percent, and that for attendance at a top-50 institution is less than 2.5 percent.

More important to the present study is the heterogeneity visible within each distribution. These differences in the probability of college-going create separation between growth rates in population and growth rates in demand for higher education. One way to measure the extent of this variation is by comparing the 25th and 75th percentile probabilities within each distribution. For the broadest measure of higher education—attendance at any postsecondary institution—the probability of attendance is approximately 50 percent at the bottom quartile and 80 percent at the top. The variation among probabilities is predictably smaller for two-year college attendance (interquartile range between 22.5 percent and 35 percent) than for four-year college attendance (interquartile range between 22.5 percent and 60 percent). However, in all three of these categories of college demand, the 75th percentile probabilities are significantly larger than those at the 25th percentile. In the case of attendance at top-100 or top-50 institutions, the interquartile range is necessarily narrower because attendance probabilities are generally so low. Still, while almost 70 percent of the population experiences a probability of attending a school ranked in the top 50 that is less than 2.5 percent, 5 percent of the population has a better than 15 percent chance of enrollment at

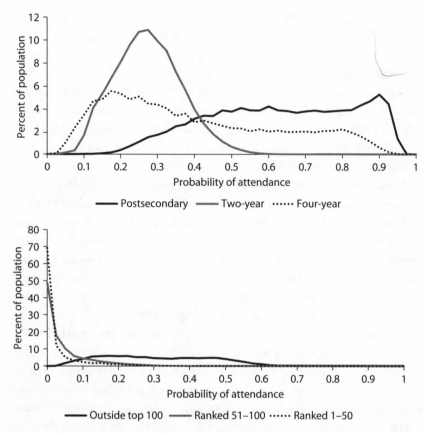

Figure 3.1. Distributions of the estimated probability of college attendance among 17-year-olds in the 2011 American Community Survey

one of these elite institutions. Because college-going probabilities are so heterogeneous, simple population forecasts alone are of limited value in predicting the demand for college.

Estimating the Number of Children by Location, Demographic Group, and Birth Cohort

Having estimated the probability of attendance for children with different geographic and demographic characteristics, the HEDI uses these estimates to weight headcounts of children observed in the ACS. This annual Census Bureau survey collects demographic information, including location, age, race/ethnicity, education, income, and place of birth. (Some readers may recognize these as items from the census long form, the contents of which were transferred from the decennial census to the annual ACS in 2001.) The ACS is administered throughout the year, with information solicited from people living at approximately 250,000 addresses each month. Over the course of a year, more than three million people are included in the survey. Drawing on data from the 2011 administration of the ACS, it is possible to estimate the number of children in each birth cohort living in that year in each of the 63 locations identified previously. These headcounts form the backbone of the model's forecasts of the number of children reaching college age in any given year.

The logic of the population model is quite simple: children get older one year at a time. For example, a 6-year-old living in Oklahoma in 2011 is quite likely to be an 18-year-old Oklahoman in 2023. Of course, reality is more complex than this. Mortality, migration, and immigration complicate the picture as children leave and enter a state's or city's population. What is more, the probability model described earlier shows large effects of family structure on children's college attendance. So, even when children remain in the same state, we must account for potential changes in their parents' marital relationship.

Adjustments for mortality are calculated using statistics reported by the Centers for Disease Control and Prevention. Multiplying a series of annual mortality rates (conditional on age and race/ethnicity) yields estimates of the probability that an observed child will live to college-going age. These survival probabilities are used to adjust the expected number of native-born children in each state from each birth cohort and demographic group. As might be expected, this correction is very slight for the population as a whole, and for all subgroups.

Migration requires larger adjustments: more than 1.5 percent of children report moving from one state to another in the year leading up to the 2011 ACS. For native-born children, the HEDI uses migration patterns observed in the ACS to project movements from the age each child is observed through age 18. Given the large number of migration patterns to estimate (63 locations of origin and destination combine to form 3,969 location pairs), sample size limitations restrict the number of variables used to explain migration. Patterns in the 2011 ACS suggest the most important predictors of migration are child's age, mother's education, and race/ethnicity. Using these factors, the HEDI predicts migration rates to estimate the probability an observed child will end up in any one of the 63 locations at college-going age.

Combining these estimated migration probabilities with the number of children observed in each location in the ACS yields an adjusted number of children expected in each location at age 18. The effect of these migration adjustments on expected future populations vary considerably by location. For example, a child living in nonmetropolitan Georgia (i.e., not in Atlanta) at age 10 has a better than 60 percent probability of changing location by age 18 if she is Hispanic or Asian and living with a mother with at least a high school diploma. By contrast, a 4-year-old Mississippian who is neither Hispanic nor Asian has a better than 95 percent chance of remaining in Mississippi at the age of college-going.

Future expected immigration necessitates similar adjustments to headcounts of nonnative children. For every young foreign-born child of a given demographic type observed in the ACS, we can expect several more similar children of the same birth cohort to arrive in the United States before that cohort reaches age 18. To account for this, the HEDI treats each nonnative child as more than one child at age 18, using observed age-population patterns within each location to predict how much nonnative population growth we might expect to occur in a given birth cohort. For example, suppose we observe three times as many foreign-born 17-year-olds as 5-year-olds of a given demographic group in a particular state. In such a case, the HEDI assumes each observed 5-year-old in this group will become three 17-year-olds in 12 years' time.[5]

Finally, even if no children die or move from one location to another, family structure may change, and so alter a child's probability of college attendance. Because the ACS only observes families at one point in time, it provides no information about changes in family structure. The HEDI uses the longitudinal Panel Study of Income Dynamics to estimate the probability of changes to family structure conditional on the mother's education. These probabilities are used to adjust the expected number of children living in each family structure type in each location in each birth cohort.

Key Assumptions

The approach laid out earlier in this chapter rests on several assumptions that should be explored to understand how future shocks could cause the projections to go awry. At a basic level, the assumptions can be summarized "the way the world works in the next few years will be much like it has in the recent past." In some dimensions, this seems very, very safe to assume. For example, it would be surprising if child mortality rates suddenly spiked. But it is less clear that other relationships between key variables will remain unchanged over time.

- **College attendance patterns.** The forecast model rests on estimates of the probability of college-going conditional on demographic characteristics and family background. For the forecasts to be reasonable, we must assume that the relationships between college-going and these explanatory variables remain constant between 2004 and 2006, when the ELS students made their choices, and 2029, when the youngest children in the ACS reach age 18. For example, if being female increases by 5 percent the probability that a member of the ELS sample attended a four-year institution, then the forecast model assumes that infant females in the ACS will experience the same probability advantage in 2029.

  So long as economic and educational environments remain stable, this seems like a reasonable assumption. However, Congress may expand or contract student loan support, the Supreme Court may change its perspective on racial preferences in admission, states may expand programs that mitigate disadvantages of growing up in low-income households, technological change may alter returns to education, or some other innovation might increase or decrease rates of college attendance in general, or for specific groups. Any of these could alter substantially the relationships between demographic characteristics and college attendance rates underlying HEDI forecasts.

  One such change may already be present in the data. As noted in chapter 2, the current generation of parents participated in a rapid expansion in college attainment. Among ACS children ages 15 to 17, only 12.8 percent report that each parent has at least a four-year degree. That figure jumps to 18.5 percent (an increase of more than 45 percent) among children younger than age 3. With such rapid expansion in higher education among parents, it is reasonable to wonder whether "being college educated" means the same thing among older and younger parents in the ACS. If the nature of parents' college educations changes over time, we might expect the effect of parental education on the probability of children's college attendance to respond accordingly.

- **Migration and immigration patterns.** Migration estimates are formed by looking backward at movements prior to the 2011 ACS. This approach will be off the mark to the degree that future migration patterns differ from those in the recent past. Of particular note, when states experience economic downturns, we often see changes to in- and out-migration. Whether this flow should be expected to continue depends on the persistence of the forces behind those difficult economic times. For example, in recent years both Michigan and southern California have seen out-migration and unemployment above the national average. The forecast model assumes that these migration patterns will continue for the next 18 years. Because the causes of economic distress differ in these two regions, we may be more or less comfortable with the assumption of constant migration rates. Work by the Pew Foundation shows that migration patterns have been more or less stable over the past 40 years.[6] Nevertheless, it is likely that some individual locations saw particularly high rates of in- or out-migration in 2011 that will not persist through the 2020s.

The assumption of stable immigration rates inherently contains the same concerns because the immigration adjustment described previously also captures within-country migration by nonnatives subsequent to arriving in the United States. In addition, immigration adjustment involves assumptions about the rate of immigrant arrival to the United States as a whole. Even if states all experienced identical economic shocks, so that there were no pressures favoring one state or city over another, the performance of the US economy as a whole may draw immigrants at a rate that is higher or lower than has been experienced in recent decades. In addition, immigration policy reform could fundamentally change incentives to immigrate in the future such that the past is a poor guide for forecasts.

The experience of higher education in the 1990s provides a useful case study on how violations of these assumptions can confound forecasts of the demand for postsecondary education. As noted in chapter 1, from 1960 to the mid-1970s the total fertility rate plummeted by approximately 50 percent (Schoen 2004). As a result, the number of births in the United States fell from around 4.25 million per year to only 3.2 million in a period only slightly longer than a decade. By 1980, most analysts predicted a looming, precipitous drop in college enrollment (Fiske 1980). Fiske notes that a few economists at the time argued the pessimistic forecasts were likely to fail because they were based on simple headcounts.

Echoing arguments made in chapter 2, these economists pointed out that increases in education in previous years foreshadowed future rises in parental education, which, in turn, would increase college attendance rates and cushion the coming enrollment drop. Furthermore, they argued that smaller families would likely choose to invest more in education because having fewer children relaxes family budget constraints.

Of course, we know now that what actually happened in the subsequent decade looked nothing like the dire predictions. Undergraduate enrollments rose from 10.5 million in 1980, to 12 million in 1990, to more than 13 million in 2000 (NCES 2015, table 303.70). Had enrollments dropped by 25 percent as births had done approximately 20 years earlier, undergraduate enrollments would have fallen to less than eight million. Undoubtedly, rising parental education and reductions in family size mitigated the effects of the birth dearth as forecasted by the contrarian analysts cited by Fiske. So, while most forecasts vastly missed their target, at the same time the experience of the 1990s represents a partial success for more careful forecast modeling.

However, economists broadly agree that these predictable factors alone cannot account for roughly 4 million added college students (the difference between the proportionate drop to 7.9 million and the actual increase to 12 million between 1980 and 1990). Instead, we believe increased investment in education was a response to a large increase in the demand for skills of all kinds flowing from technological changes that increased the relative returns to those skills. This well-examined phenomenon is confirmed in a large number of empirical studies, with the most commonly cited evidence being the rapid increase in the returns to college education observed during the 1980s. Drawing on data from the US Census Bureau, Goldin and Katz (2008, appendix D) estimate that college graduates enjoyed a 20 percent wage premium relative to those holding a high school diploma in 1950. Their study finds that this advantage changed only slightly for the following three decades. However, during the 1980s the college wage premium nearly tripled, to 55 percent, peaking at more than 60 percent by 1990 before falling back slightly, to 57 percent, by 2004.[7] This dramatic increase in price for skilled labor occurred despite a rapid increase in the number and proportion of workers holding a college degree, signaling a strong rise in demand for skilled labor. In light of this surge in demand for skilled workers, it is not surprising that higher education institutions managed to maintain enrollments despite the smaller pool of potential students. Larger shares of high school graduates continued on to postsecondary education, and older, "nontraditional" students returned to the classroom to acquire additional training and tap into these higher rewards.

Because skill-biased technical change was unpredicted (and perhaps unpredictable) in the 1970s, the rise in postsecondary enrollment in the subsequent decades largely represents a failure for forecasting. This failure offers several important lessons for the present work. First, it underscores the fact that forward-looking forecasts are inevitably grounded in backward-looking analysis. Because, by definition, we cannot fully foresee future shocks and paradigm shifts, forecast models necessarily assume the world tomorrow will reflect facts and patterns seen today. Indeed, to the extent the world is literally unpredictable, we must accept that projections will err. Forecasting involves a healthy dose of humility.

This is not to say that forecasts can only predict a future "just like today." Just as economists in the 1980s anticipated that rising parental education would lead to higher college attendance rates, it is possible to anticipate future changes flowing from patterns observable in the present. Ignoring this potential out of fear that an unforeseeable paradigm shift might be around the corner leaves education policymakers without information critical to their work. Our inability to foresee perfectly should not be an argument against looking ahead.

Finally, even as the change in returns to education during the 1980s gives rise to caution concerning the assumptions inherent to any forecasting model, the otherwise-stable returns to education from 1950 to 1980 and from 1990 to 2005 provide reason for optimism. While the earth does sometimes shift beneath our feet, such occurrences are relatively rare. In particular, given that returns to education are currently elevated, it seems reasonable to assume that we will not experience a second surge that overcomes the present birth dearth. Indeed, some researchers argue that since 2000 we have entered a period with decreasing returns to skill (Beaudry et al. 2016). If that is the case, and if the pattern is extensive, then demand may fall short of forecasts as economic conditions amplify rather than offset demographic changes as they did in the 1990s.

Evaluating the Forecast Model

Before applying the HEDI to questions of the future, we should test its efficacy by asking it to answer questions from the past for which we already know the answers. Specifically, this section tests the quality of the model's forecasts by applying the HEDI to data from the 2000 Census to form predictions of subsequently observed populations and levels of college attendance. Because population estimates form the foundation for enrollment projections, I begin there. Children observed between the ages of 4 and 6 years old in the 2000 Census are drawn from the same population as those between 15 and 17 years of age in the 2011 ACS. To clarify the source of the forecast model's power, I consider two population predictions. The first is a baseline model that sets the 2011 population estimate equal to the observed 2000 Census population with no adjustments; that is, the number of 15- to 17-year-olds in a location in 2011 is estimated to be the number of 4- to 6-year-olds in that same location in 2000. The second, full model applies the previously noted corrections with a modest revision for the fact that in the model evaluation, the population is of age 16 on average rather than college-going age.

Figure 3.2 plots the population predictions of the baseline (stars) and full (circles) models (based on figures in the 2000 Census) against the numbers of children ages 15 to 17 reported in the 2011 ACS. Each point represents 1 of 63 cities and nonmetropolitan portions of states. The upper panel of the figure shows data for all locations, while the lower panel zooms in on the large mass of lower-population locations, excluding (from largest to smallest) observations from New York City, Los Angeles, nonmetropolitan Texas, and Chicago. The strong relationship between the observed populations and baseline (stars) predictions points to the power of the basic logic behind the population forecast model: despite the complexities of migration, immigration, and mortality, the population of young children in a particular state is a strong predictor of 18-year-olds a decade hence.

While the figure (particularly panel b) shows that the full model outperforms the baseline, we can quantify the errors by summing absolute discrepancies between actual and predicted populations. In the country as a whole, the baseline model underestimates the population by 733,000 children, or 5.8 percent of the total number observed in the 2011 ACS.[8] This shortfall stems from the model's failure to account for immigration. By contrast, the full model misses the nationwide population by only 231,000, or 1.8 percent, a 70 percent reduction in the error rate.

While accurately predicting the aggregate size of future cohorts is important, because institutions draw from very different geographies, it is also important to forecast populations in more narrowly defined geographic areas such as metropolitan areas, states, and census divisions. Not surprisingly, the sum of absolute errors generally grows as geographic granularity increases. Because the baseline model underpredicts populations in each and every census division, the sum of absolute errors across census divisions equals that in the country as a

a) All locations

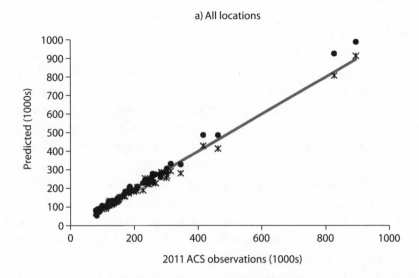

b) Locations with populations fewer than 500,000

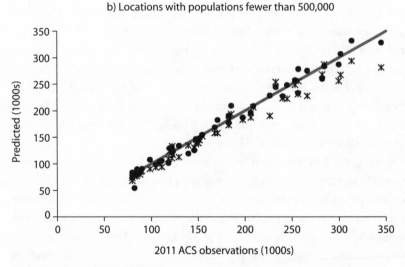

Figure 3.2. HEDI predictions of 15- to 17-year-olds in 2011 versus observed. *Note:* The baseline model (stars) predicts 15- to 17-year-old populations based on Census 2000 counts of children ages 4 to 6 without adjustment. The full model (circles) adjusts for mortality, migration, and immigration. The solid line denotes perfect agreement between the model predictions and 2011 American Community Survey observations.

whole—5.8 percent. Similarly, as we increase geographic granularity to the level of census division, the error rate for the full model increases slightly—to 2.6 percent. At the highest level of geographical granularity, predicting populations at the level of state or metropolitan area, the baseline and full models post error rates of 7.2 percent and 6.6 percent, respectively. On the whole, the models do a reasonable job of predicting populations of children nearing college-going age over a 10-year horizon.[9] So, if all we cared about were future populations of young adults, headcounts of current young children would be a reasonable proxy.

However, as we see from the argument made in the previous chapter, accurate population projections are insufficient for enrollment forecasts. The NCES's *Digest of Education Statistics* records by-state estimates of the number of students who enroll in the fall for the first time at a degree-granting postsecondary institution (table 305.20). These data differ conceptually from HEDI forecasts in three important ways. First, the NCES estimates the number of students who matriculate in a given year, while the model predicts college attendance among those who graduate in a given high school cohort. For example, if a student was born in the high school class of 2003 but did not start college until 2005, the NCES includes that student in its 2005 figures, while the forecast model counts that student with the 2003 cohort. So long as the number of students delaying entrance to college remains constant over time, this difference in accounting cancels out across cohorts. However, because the number of individuals going back to school moves counter to the economic cycle, we expect that some cohorts delay more than others, and so this difference in definition will create divergence between HEDI forecasts and NCES observations.

Second, the locations used in the forecast model do not map exactly onto states. First, states were sometimes combined to achieve a population of two million. Moreover, metropolitan areas sometimes cross state lines. For comparison's sake, I combine areas in the HEDI and the NCES *Digest* to reach a common denominator.[10] It should be noted that a few geographical discrepancies remain. In particular, the Chicago, Cincinnati, Kansas City, Minneapolis–St. Paul, Philadelphia, and St. Louis metropolitan areas have populations that fall across state lines and were assigned, respectively, to Illinois, Ohio, Kansas, Minnesota, Pennsylvania, and Missouri.[11] The state of New Jersey poses larger problems. All of that state falls in either the New York City or Philadelphia metropolitan areas, but it is impossible to parse the New Jersey population in the NCES's state-based report. Two choices present themselves: combine all of New York and Pennsylvania into a single location or assign NCES observations from New Jersey to only one of those two states and accept the resulting error. Because New York and Pennsylvania are large sources of college students, I followed the latter policy and combined New Jersey with New York.

Finally (and most fundamentally), the NCES records the state in which a student enrolls in college, while the model speaks to the state in which the student resided in high school. To the degree to which some states import (export) more students than they export (import), HEDI forecasts cannot be expected to match the NCES data. The NCES reports the ratio of in-state students to first-time postsecondary enrollment in the year 2014 for the 50 states and the District of Columbia (NCES 2015, table 309.10). Across the 50 states and the District, this ratio averages 0.79. At the positive extreme, only Texas and New Jersey posted a ratio exceeding 0.90. On the other extreme, in-state first-year enrollment in Vermont represented just 33 percent of all first-year students in that state. The District of Columbia brought up the rear with only 9 percent of first-time college students studying there hailing from the District.

These differences in data definitions introduce inherent discrepancies between NCES reports and HEDI projections. Despite this bias against the model, the projections match the enrollment data well. Figure 3.3 plots HEDI predictions of college attendance five years ahead against NCES reports of actual enrollments. The correlation between NCES figures and the model's predictions is greater than 0.96. The best-fit line (dashed line) runs very close to the 45-degree line of perfect prediction (and this is particularly true at the heart of the scatter, where most observations are found). The sum of absolute difference across the 35 locations is around 350,000, or 13 percent of the total number of college entrants estimated by the NCES. Given significant differences in data definitions, this degree of fit suggests the model has reasonable power in predicting enrollments.

Next, I compare NCES reports of first-time college attenders in 2012, a dozen years after the 2000 Census, with HEDI predictions. Figure 3.4 plots the results. The degree of match between the forecasts and the NCES figures of actual attendance is quite similar to that when forecasting five years out. The correlation is slightly higher at this longer forecast range (0.97), though the dashed line of best fit now runs visibly below, and parallel to, the solid line of perfect prediction. This indicates that the HEDI model consistently underestimates enrollments. The systematic error might be understood in light of the financial crisis that began in 2008 and continues to affect labor markets today. With unusually few opportunities available on the job market, the rate of college attendance in that period exceeded what would be expected in more normal times. In these

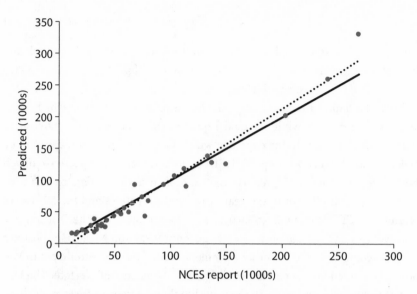

Figure 3.3. HEDI predictions of first-time college attenders in 2005 versus observed. *Note:* The dashed line represents the line of best fit running through the data, while the solid line represents perfect agreement between the model predictions and 2005 NCES observations. *Source:* NCES reports are taken from the 2013 Digest of Education Statistics, table 305.20.

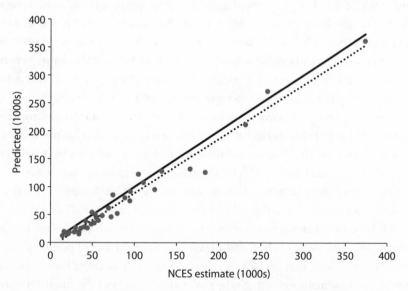

Figure 3.4. HEDI predictions of first-time college attenders in 2012 versus observed. *Note:* The dashed line represents the line of best fit running through the data, while the solid line represents perfect agreement between the model predictions and 2005 NCES observations. *Source:* NCES reports are taken from the 2013 Digest of Education Statistics, table 305.20.

exceptional circumstances, the total sum of errors across locations is around 475,000, or 16 percent of college entrants reported by the NCES. Even as the discrepancies—fueled in part by the Great Recession—remind us once more of the limitations and assumptions inherent in any forecasting exercise, the general quality of match is very strong in an era of rapid enrollment expansion (up 24 percent nationally) and despite significant differences in data definitions between the HEDI forecasts and the NCES comparison data.

Having developed the HEDI and established its forecasting capacity, expected changes in higher education demand can be studied in aggregate and by subgroups. In particular, the following chapters assess predictions of the dominant narrative concerning trends in demand and shifts across geographic and racial/ethnic subparts of the population. Not surprisingly, demand for college defined in the broadest sense is expected to follow the path called out in the headlines. But when the industry is divided along lines of institutional type, very different stories emerge. As a result, some colleges and universities may wish to think carefully before settling on new recruitment strategies and pedagogies designed to meet coming demographic changes.

Chapter Four

Changing Contours of Population and Aggregate Higher Education Demand

The first application of the Higher Education Demand Index will be to the broadest measures of potential demand: college-aged population and postsecondary enrollment. The argument made in earlier chapters is that the breadth of these measures makes them of relatively little use to institutional decision makers. Nevertheless, the forecasts presented in this chapter serve three purposes. First, some national policy questions are informed by these large aggregates. For example, concerns about rising income inequality may lead to expansions of subsidies with the goal of increasing college attendance rates. Second, these broad measures serve as a baseline of comparison for subsequent chapters devoted to subsectors of the higher education industry. Having read numerous stories—if not formal studies—describing demographic change, many readers will have a general sense of forecasted changes in population. The maps and figures presented in this chapter transform that general feeling into a detailed understanding. Armed with this reference point, readers can appreciate more fully subsequent estimates of growth or loss in demand for two-year colleges or elite institutions presented in later chapters—and how those changes are consistent or at odds with predictions of dramatic geographic and racial/ethnic change.

Third, and perhaps most importantly, projections of broad population and college-going numbers provide a point of comparison with widely known projections of the Western Interstate Commission for Higher Education (WICHE) presented in chapter 1. As the next sections show, the HEDI forecasts of population and college-going are broadly consistent with WICHE projections for high school graduation. This similarity clarifies the source of differences between WICHE and HEDI estimates presented in subsequent chapters. Because the two models generally agree on broad population movements, when HEDI predictions for subsectors of higher education differ from the dominant narrative, the cause of the variation lies in the way the HEDI accounts for college-going probabilities.

National Forecasts

Based on experiences recorded in the 2002 Education Longitudinal Study, we expect more than 70 percent of young people to acquire some postsecondary education within two years of high school completion. Given such a high rate of uptake, this broadest measure of higher education demand, by construction, must walk (more or less) in lockstep with population projections. According to HEDI estimates presented in figure 4.1, both population and college-going students are expected to hold steady through the early 2020s before a brief and modest 5 percent increase precedes a precipitous reduction of 15 percent or more. The reduction in population and higher education demand at the end of this period is staggering. In the half decade beginning in 2025, the HEDI predicts that the cohort size of 18-year-olds will shrink more than 650,000, while the number of first-time college-goers contracts by nearly 450,000. Since several cohorts attend college in any given year, the aggregate effect on enrollments will be several times as large.

It is difficult to grasp the meaning of these forecasts without placing them in historical context. After about 30 years of steady growth, echoes of the fertility reductions of the 1960s pushed first-time enrollments down by 18 percent over a dozen or so years, beginning in 1980 (National Center for Education Statistics 2015, table 305.10).[1] The projections presented in figure 4.1 suggest we might expect a similarly deep contraction accomplished in only half a decade. Alternatively, we might compare the coming enrollment crunch to a more recent experience: between 2009 and 2012, first-time enrollments fell not quite 7 percent. Over a similar time span, the model expects the pullback of the late 2020s to be twice as large. Unless something unexpected intervenes, the confluence of current demographic changes foretells an unprecedented reduction in postsecondary education demand about a decade ahead.

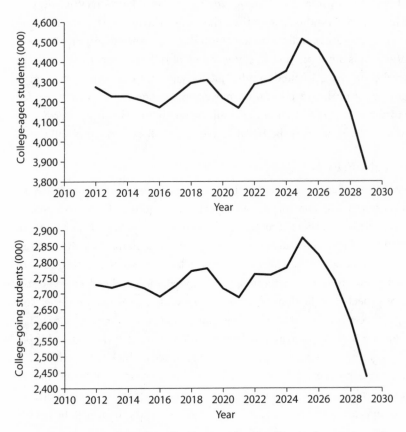

Figure 4.1. Forecasted number of college-aged and college-going students, by year of high school graduation

Local Forecasts

While the national forecast is critical for some questions (e.g., the late 2020s look to be a very poor time to be seeking a teaching post in higher education), the health of most institutions rests on regional or local conditions to which we now turn. At four-year public institutions, more than 80 percent of students claim in-state status, and at two-year schools that figure tops 90 percent (Kumar and Hurwitz 2015). The fraction of in-state students at flagship public institutions is notably lower, near 65 percent, and has been trending downward in recent years. Still, a majority of students at these schools originate in-state. When college-going forecasts are broken down by census division, the Mountain and West

South Central divisions are clear, positive outliers, expected to experience growth of 15 to 25 percent by 2025, before the effects of the birth dearth return postsecondary demand more or less to the levels of today.[2] The South Atlantic is expected to experience only modest change throughout the forecast period. The remaining divisions, which account for more than 60 percent of 18-year-olds and a slightly higher share of postsecondary enrollees, are expected to follow various paths of collapse, ranging from painful, down approximately 10 percent in the Pacific and West North Central, to highly disruptive, off almost 20 percent everywhere else, with the exception of New England, which anticipates a 25 percent loss.

The disruption caused by divisional losses will be amplified by the fact that the areas of greatest loss tend to be those with the highest postsecondary enrollment rates (correlation = 0.66). In other words, the largest reductions in student numbers will occur in divisions with large numbers of regional institutions and the greatest recruitment networks among national schools. For example, while the growth expected in the Mountain West and West South Central looks promising, the rise comes off a small base because these divisions send relatively few students to college. By contrast, we expect deep contraction in midwestern and northeastern divisions that send high proportions of students to higher education. This correlation amplifies concerns for higher education demand when changes are viewed in absolute, rather than relative, terms. On a divisional level, the East North Central (the largest loser) expects to lose 12 times as many college-going students as the West South Central (the largest winner) is predicted to gain. Tellingly, the many divisional losses are measured in tens of thousands, while the few gains (in the Mountain and West South Central) are an order of magnitude smaller. A similar pattern is seen at the local level, though the ratio of losses to gains is smaller. For example, the predicted losses in New York City, the location of greatest loss, are three times as large as the gains in Houston, the area of largest gain. This three-to-one ratio is generalizable to other areas of great gains and losses.

The reason the ratio of losses to gains is larger across divisions than across metropolitan areas / states is that gains and losses show strong spatial correlation: locations that are close in geographical proximity face similar future changes to population and college-going. This is clearly evident in figures 4.2 and 4.3, which map predicted growth rates for population and postsecondary enrollment on a local level. From the study of population, only a handful of bright spots emerge, most in the Mountain West or South (figure 4.2). With the exception of Minnesota and

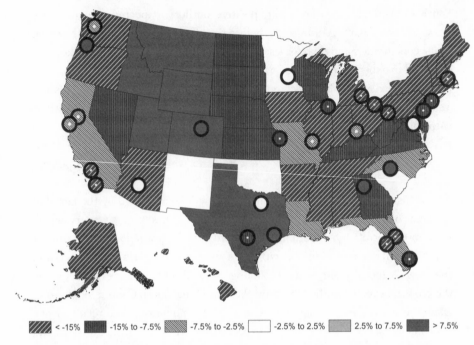

 <-15%   -15% to -7.5%   -7.5% to -2.5%   ☐ -2.5% to 2.5%   ▨ 2.5% to 7.5%   ■ > 7.5%

Figure 4.2. Forecasted growth in 18-year-olds, 2012 to 2029

Minneapolis–St. Paul, every location in the Northeast and Midwest expects fewer 18-year-olds in 2029 than today. Atlanta and Charlotte represent the only hopes for noticeable growth east of the Mississippi River.

When population figures are adjusted for the probability of college-going (figure 4.3), the situation looks a bit worse in two-thirds of the locations. In the northeast quadrant of the country, Minnesota and Minneapolis–St. Paul join all the other locations in expected contraction. Moreover, the large markets in New York City and Philadelphia join Boston in posting dramatic losses of 15 percent or greater. Of all 63 locations, only South Carolina shows meaningfully more growth in college-going than in college-aged population—an increase in expected growth rate from about 1.5 percent in population to just more than 5 percent in postsecondary demand. Overall, the maps of HEDI forecasts for population and postsecondary enrollment conform to the pessimistic narrative concerning higher education's future.

In addition to looking at divisions or specific locations, the HEDI can also be used to anticipate trends in urbanization. The 28 metropolitan areas in the study account for 49.5 percent of the 2012 college-aged population. The HEDI

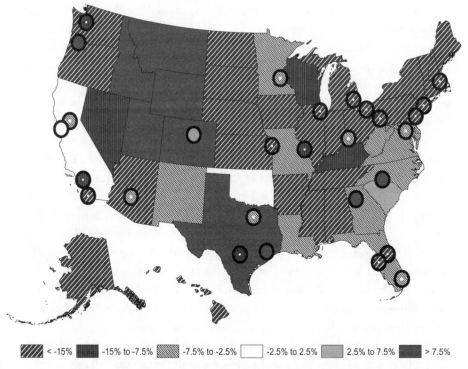

 Figure 4.3. Forecasted growth in college-going students, 2012 to 2029

suggests little change in this distribution by 2029, when 50.3 percent of 18-year-olds are projected to live in a metropolitan area. Due to the nature of the HEDI's construction, it is not surprising that the model projects relatively little variation in urbanization in the population. The primary factors that could cause a change in this measure are rates of immigration to and migration in/out of metropolitan areas. Because the model projects future immigration and migration based on the experience of the recent past, and because we are not currently seeing massive net movements toward or away from urban centers, the projections could not have been otherwise. For the same reason, it is unsurprising that the representation of metropolitan areas in the demand for higher education, while slightly higher than in the population as a whole, is expected to be more or less flat, rising from 51.9 percent to 52.3 percent. (The modest shift results from the fact that demand in metropolitan areas is expected to contract by 10 percent, while that in nonmetropolitan locations falls by 12 points.)

The relative stability of urban share at the national level is also predicted within census divisions. This is interesting because the divisions vary widely in the degree of urbanness of their college-aged populations. In 2012, the predicted share of young adults hailing from metropolitan areas ranged from 0 percent in the East South Central (where there are no major metropolitan areas) to 75 percent in the Pacific. Despite these differences, the Pacific, Mountain, East North Central, and South Atlantic each anticipate a change of less than one percentage point in the urban share of 18-year-olds. The largest increase in urbanization is expected in the Middle Atlantic—a rise of 1.8 percentage points. The HEDI predicts even smaller interregional variation in urbanization trends among the college-going population. Only the Middle Atlantic expects an urban share in 2029 that is more than one percentage point different than that in 2012, and even there the college-going cohort is only predicted to grow by 1.5 points. Thus, while the HEDI suggests no reversal to urbanization trends, in no part of the country does the model foresee a dramatic acceleration in urbanization between now and 2029. While these predictions of stable urbanization in the broad college-aged and college-going populations are unremarkable in and of themselves, they will be an important baseline for comparison in later discussions.

As noted previously, the broad similarity between projections for population and college-going in figures 4.2 and 4.3 follows from the fact that a large majority of young people acquire some postsecondary education, and so this broadest definition of college demand can be driven by little else than underlying population trends. This is also true of changes in population and college demand within demographic subgroups. Figure 4.4 shows that the racial/ethnic makeup of the nation is expected to shift dramatically over the next few years. Specifically, the number of non-Hispanic whites reaching college age is projected to fall by more than 15 percent in vast swaths of the country and to grow almost nowhere. Only a pocket in the Mountain West promises anything like region-wide growth. Non-Hispanic blacks are expected to grow in number in some nonmetropolitan portions of states, particularly in the West. However, the HEDI predicts contraction in every city but San Antonio, Houston, and Philadelphia. By contrast, students identifying as Hispanic or Asian American will increase robustly in all but a few locations. While a few West Coast cities stand out as important exceptions, as a group higher education institutions can expect larger numbers of Asian and Hispanic students in recruitment pools in all regions of the country.

Differences in growth rates are even more dramatic when the population is divided by levels of parental education, as shown in figure 4.5. In a handful of

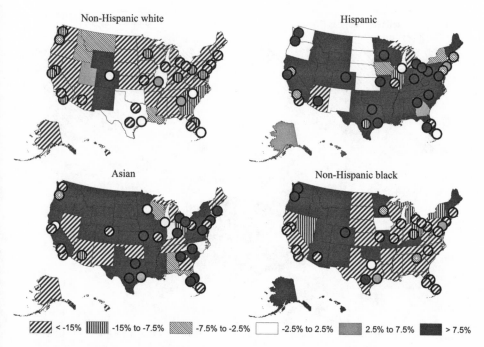

Figure 4.4. Forecasted growth in 18-year-olds by race/ethnicity, 2012 to 2029

locations, the number of young people with no model of a parental bachelor's degree ("first-generation students") will increase. These areas tend to be in pockets where aggregate population is expected to increase such that the rise in overall numbers of young people overcomes the decreasing share of first-generation students. However, the strong trend toward greater education across generations of parents generally dominates: with exceptions in Illinois and nonmetropolitan New England, the entire country expects robust growth in the numbers of potential students with deep levels of parental education. This is all the more remarkable when we recall that this increase plays out despite significant contraction in the population as a whole.

Because this forecast is entirely at odds with the headline predictions of ever-increasing numbers of first-generation students, it seems necessary to pause and ask why that might be. One possibility is that headline stories conflate the shifts seen along lines of race/ethnicity with those in parental education. Perhaps analysts see rising Hispanic populations, note the historically lower levels of college attendance among that subgroup, and conclude that first-generation students

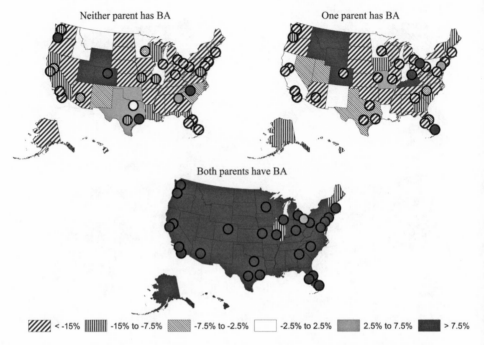

Figure 4.5. Forecasted growth in 18-year-olds by parental education, 2012 to 2029

must be on the rise. (Of course, at the same time, the number of Asian Americans is also increasing, and this group has had exceptionally strong attachments to higher education.) Alternatively, analysts may be extrapolating from past experiences. As college attendance rates have risen over the past century, we have naturally seen large and increasing numbers of first-generation students acquire degrees. It might be natural to expect such an established trend to continue. Perhaps the most likely explanation for this disconnect stems from the disproportionate attention paid to elite institutions, which, as chapter 6 explores more fully, are expected to be outliers in many dimensions. Unlike every other institution group, elite institutions will see greater demand generated by first-generation students—an increase of more than 10 percent. Even among these elites, demand will grow much faster among students whose parents have deeper educational backgrounds so that the share of first-generation students will fall. Still, it may be that analysts' eyes are drawn to the growing absolute numbers at prominent institutions. Whatever the explanation, the dominant story in which future campuses teach increasing numbers and shares of first-generation students is inconsistent with the data.

While the differences in projected population trends across race/ethnicity and parental education shown in figures 4.4 and 4.5 are sizable, recall that projections for population and postsecondary enrollment are incredibly similar. The strong resemblance between trends in population and broad postsecondary demand means that nearly all of the predicted change in broadly defined postsecondary enrollment is explained by changes in aggregate population. While chapter 2 noted meaningful absolute differences in postsecondary enrollment rates by race/ethnicity and parental education, postsecondary enrollment rates are high enough for all groups such that relative differences in broad "college attendance" are too small to revise the narrative written by population change. In other words, while careful study of demographic subgroups is essential for projections of demand for subsectors of higher education, for broad postsecondary enrollment, demographics really is destiny.

The Changing Face of Higher Education

Next, we examine the implied demographic shares of the general and college-going populations. Perhaps surprisingly, despite large differences in growth rates in population across regions, the model predicts only modest effects on the geographic makeup of college-bound students in coming years. Figure 4.6 presents expected geographic distributions of the college-aged and college-going today and in 2029. An increase of two percentage points in the share of college students from the South Atlantic will mirror a drop of two percentage points in the share from the Midwest, but all other shares in 2029 are predicted to be within one percentage point of 2012 shares. The reason for the general stasis is simple: nearly all regions, cities, and nonurban portions of states are shrinking, and the few exceptions currently contribute only modest numbers of college students. Even fast growth from a small base amounts to little absolute change, and so the geographic distribution of the nation's college students is expected to remain largely unaltered despite substantial drops in overall enrollment levels.

By contrast, the data in figure 4.7 show that the distribution of college students across race/ethnicity will shift noticeably in the next 15 years. The share of non-Hispanic white and non-Hispanic black college students will closely follow shares in the 18-year-old population, falling approximately 10 percentage points. Half or more of this reduced share is attributable to the five-point increase in the Hispanic share, with the remainder accounted for by smaller increases in the

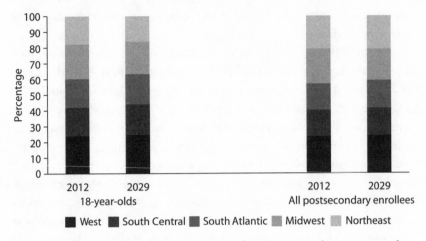

Figure 4.6. Forecasted geographic distribution of students attending postsecondary institutions, 2012 and 2029

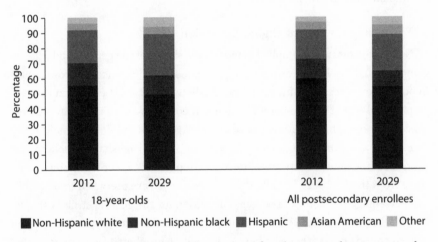

Figure 4.7. Forecasted race/ethnicity distribution of students attending postsecondary institutions, 2012 and 2029

shares of Asian American and Other students. While non-Hispanic whites make up a clear majority of college students in 2012 (60 percent), that majority will be much slimmer in 2029 (less than 55 percent of postsecondary enrollees). Arguably, the most noticeable change will be found among non-Hispanic blacks. Even though the share of students in this group is predicted to fall by only three percentage points (half the magnitude of the reduction in share for non-Hispanic whites), this represents a fall of more than 20 percent from today, when these

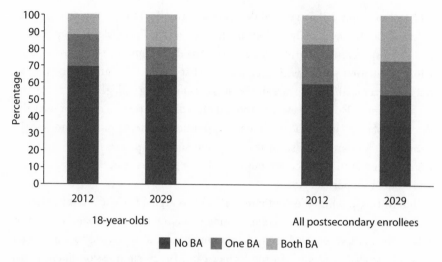

Figure 4.8. Forecasted parental education distribution of students attending postsecondary institutions, 2012 and 2029

students make up 13 percent of the whole. Taken together, it is unclear whether, on net, the nation's college student body will feel more or less diverse.

As previously noted, the rise in college attainment over recent decades fore-shadows greater college attainment among parent generations. Not only are students with educated parents growing in number, but they are gaining in their population share. Figure 4.8 graphs HEDI predictions reflecting this shift. Contrary to popular perception, the share of 18-year-olds with no parental model of four-year college completion will fall five percentage points. This reduction will be offset by an increase in the share of students with strong family education backgrounds: the share of young people in families with two parental bachelor's degrees will increase seven points—up more than 50 percent from the current share. Due to the strong correlation between parent and child educational acquisition, these shifts will be even more evident among postsecondary enrollees. While first-generation students make up a clear majority (60 percent) of postsecondary students today, by 2029 such students will comprise just 53 percent of the whole, and more than 25 percent of college students will hail from homes with two bachelor's degrees.

The Big Picture

The fact that such a large share (70 percent) of the population acquires some postsecondary education means that the market for higher education as a whole will almost surely follow general demographic trends. This perspective justifies much of the standard analysis, such as that behind the *Chronicle of Higher Education* stories referenced earlier. A near nationwide collapse of the non-Hispanic white population paired with increases in Hispanic and Asian populations all but ensure a racial/ethnic shift among students pursuing college education in the broadest sense. However, even as these high-profile stories correctly predict the direction of shifts in the race/ethnicity distribution, the tenor of those stories still seems off. Will an increase in the Hispanic share of postsecondary enrollees from 19 percent to 24 percent require wholesale rethinking of teaching methods and student support services?

Interestingly, while the dominant narrative is arguably right about the future racial/ethnic composition of college students defined in the broadest sense, it misses the mark when predicting changes in distributions across geographic and parental education groups. In the former case, the misimpression likely stems from confusing fast growth rates for large absolute growth. Because the few areas that are expected to grow (i.e., nonurban Texas and the Mountain West) have relatively small current populations, it is difficult to imagine that future educators will notice a significant geographic shift in the nation's college students in coming years. It is more difficult to explain why so many pages have been written about the coming rise of first-generation students. Perhaps analysts making this prediction are so focused on the rising Hispanic population (which has historically had low college attendance rates) that they have missed the importance of the recent rise in educational attainment (experienced disproportionately in the Hispanic population) and its implications for the distribution of parental education in the future.

Chapter 8 considers in great detail the possible institutional responses to the enrollment shifts, but while the figures are fresh in mind it might be useful to place them in context by considering implied changes to the demand for college professors. We can get a crude sense of how many fewer faculty positions will be needed in 2029 as compared with today by looking at current student-to-faculty ratios. The National Center for Education Statistics' 2015 *Digest of Education Statistics* reports that there were 791,000 full-time and 753,000 part-time faculty working at degree-granting institutions in 2013 (table 315.10). If part-time faculty are 0.6 full-time equivalents (FTE), that makes 1.24 million FTE. The fall 2012 enrollment at these same institutions totaled 22.54 million students.[3] This puts the national student-to-faculty ratio around 18 to 1. Based on this estimate, the projected loss of 450,000 students in the second half of the 2020s corresponds to roughly 25,000 faculty positions.[4]

Recognizing that most institutions draw from regional or local pools of prospective students, we might drill down further by census division. For example, the East North Central anticipates 90,400 fewer students in 2029 than today, implying a potential reduction of nearly 5,000 faculty FTE. By contrast, growth of 7,400 enrollees in the West South Central may generate 400 new hires. However, such analysis is of questionable relevance given that we have not distinguished between institutional types. Are the reductions in students going to be felt at two-year or four-year institutions? If the latter, by national colleges and universities or by those with regional student bases? And how will demographic changes regarding race/ethnicity and parental education interact with location and institution type? These questions are taken up in the following chapters.

What is clear from the projections presented in this chapter (which conceptually mimic others' forecasts of population or high school completion) is that change is coming. For example, because it will be difficult to eliminate 25,000 faculty positions in the four years beginning in 2025, we might anticipate a steady continuation of the movement away from tenure. Similarly, we might predict no abatement in conversations about how best to recruit and serve students of Hispanic ethnicity. But beyond these very crude observations, it is difficult to make much meaning from data that lump all postsecondary students into a single category. Results of such projections are likely to be entirely unrepresentative of most institutions. If we want sound guidance for institutions of varying types, we need projections pertinent to specific institutional categories. The next chapters fill this gap in the literature.

Chapter Five

Demand for Two-Year Programs

Having established baseline predictions for the college-aged and broad college-going populations, we can now use the Higher Education Demand Index for its true purpose: to construct a more refined analysis based on college-going probabilities applied to more narrowly defined institutional groups, beginning with predictions for two-year colleges. This subset of the higher education industry has contributed more than proportionately to the increase in college attendance during the past three decades. Since 1973, the earliest date for which the National Center for Education Statistics (NCES) reports figures, the share of students enrolled in a two-year college in the October following high school completion has nearly doubled, from just less than 15 percent to more than 25 percent (NCES 2016, table 302.10). During the same period, four-year college enrollment rates among recent high school completers also increased, but by less than half (from just more than 30 percent to 44 percent). Of particular note, since the mid-1990s enrollment rates at four-year institutions leveled off, while those at two-year colleges have continued upward, reaching a record high in 2012, the final year of available data. Because four-year enrollment rates continued to rise during this period, it seems likely that two-year colleges are increasingly used as the entry point to a four-year degree. In all, nearly seven million students study at two-year institutions each year (NCES 2015, table 303.25). During the next two decades, as the effects of the birth dearth and other demographic changes are felt in higher education, how will the demand for two-year college education change, and how might we expect the demographic makeup of two-year students to evolve?

National Forecasts

While two-year college recruitment markets are quite localized, to understand developments in the sector as a whole, it is useful to begin again with national trends. The general shrinking of the college-aged population seen in chapter 4 is echoed in forecasts of two-year enrollments. The national forecast plotted in figure 5.1 shows that expected growth in two-year enrollments is actually a bit worse than that for the college-aged population as a whole. This prediction follows from the upward drift in rates of parental experience with higher education, which in turn increases the probability that students will attend four-year institutions rather than two-year competitors. With the exception of 2025, in no year is the number of two-year college-going students expected to be more than 2 percent higher than the present. Moreover, while the birth dearth will cut the 18-year-old population by 10 percent, the number of two-year college-enrolling students is expected to experience a disproportionate share of this change, dropping by 13 percent. The brief and modest reprieve in the mid-2020s will only exacerbate the ultimate fall, as enrollments plummet by 16 percent in just four years.

Even before two-year institutions realize falling enrollments due to the birth dearth, other demographic trends will transform the makeup of the national

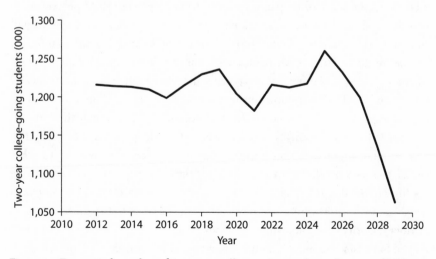

Figure 5.1. Forecasted number of two-year college-going students, by year of high school graduation

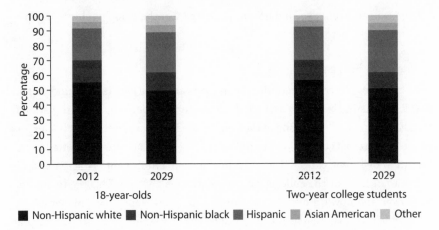

Figure 5.2. Forecasted race/ethnicity distribution of students attending two-year institutions, 2012 and 2029

population of their students. Figure 5.2 plots the expected change in the distribution of two-year college students across racial/ethnic groups. Changes along this dimension in the two-year college student body will closely mimic changes seen in the population as a whole (represented in the leftmost columns). According to the HEDI, the share of students who are non-Hispanic whites will fall by five percentage points, to just about half of all students, while the share of Hispanic students will rise by an equal or greater degree. This amounts to a 25 percent increase in the share of Hispanic students, from 22 percent to 28 percent of all two-year college enrollees. At the same time, roughly two percentage points will shift from the non-Hispanic black share to that of Asian American and Other. The net result will be that Hispanics, who make up approximately half of minority students at two-year institutions today, will become a distinct majority (nearly 60 percent) of all minority students by the end of the 2020s. The second-largest minority group, non-Hispanic blacks, will account for only one-fifth of all minorities. While these changes mirror movements in the population at large, they will be more pronounced on two-year campuses across the country. In other words, the nationwide two-year college population is expected to evolve along the lines of the dominant narrative—only more so—toward a diverse campus in which non-Hispanic whites are no longer a majority and Hispanics become a distinct majority of the nonwhite subpopulation.

The forecasts presented in figure 5.3 suggest that two-year student characteristics will also shift along the lines of parental education, but as in the popula-

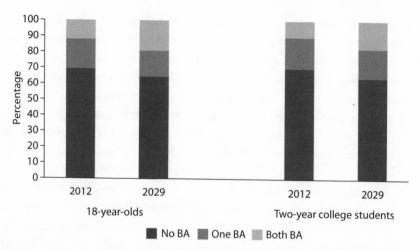

Figure 5.3. Forecasted parental education distribution of students attending two-year institutions, 2012 and 2029

tion at large the movement will be opposite that in the popular narrative. A distinct majority (70 percent) of current students come from families in which neither parent holds a bachelor's degree. In the country as a whole, first-generation students will continue to make up a majority of two-year college students in 2029, but their share within the two-year college population will fall to just less than two-thirds. This change can be broken into two parts. First, the HEDI anticipates an absolute reduction of 150,000 first-generation young people studying at two-year institutions (a 20 percent decline). At the same time, the shift in the parental education distribution will produce a 60,000-person increase in the number of entering two-year students drawn from homes in which both parents hold a four-year degree—a 45 percent increase in such students on two-year campuses. Thus, while many two-year colleges may continue to find it important to emphasize pedagogical strategies that address the particular needs of the first-generation students who make up a majority of their classes, in both relative and absolute terms, the coming demographic changes will nudge two-year student bodies toward greater family connection to higher education.

Local Forecasts

While these national forecasts provide useful context, two-year college recruitment and labor market placement tend to be highly localized. Kumar and Hurwitz (2015) estimate that around 90 percent of two-year students are drawn from within the same state as the school. But even this statistic fails to capture the local nature of two-year markets. Based on the experiences of individuals sampled in the 2002 Education Longitudinal Study (ELS), the median distance between a student's high school and an attended two-year college falls short of 15 miles (with an inter-quartile range of 7 and 35 miles).[1] Thus a large majority of two-year students attend an institution in the same metropolitan area or nonmetropolitan portion of a state as their high school. Without local projections, the national figures provide little direct guidance to administrators leading two-year institutions.

Looking across divisions, we see one important commonality: all nine geographic areas figure to bear the mark of the birth dearth, though for some divisions this represents a reversal from a positive trend, while others experience it as an increased rate of decline.[2] Aside from this important commonality, the larger story is heterogeneity. The Mountain West and West South Central expect a bit of a roller-coaster ride, with healthy increases in demand through the mid-2020s followed by a reversal to current levels in the second half of that decade. The divisions running up the East and West Coasts will hold more or less steady until 2025, when the birth dearth will reduce enrollments modestly (5 percent) in the South Atlantic and aggressively (13 and 17 percent, respectively) in New England and the Pacific. In the heart of the country—the East North Central, Middle Atlantic, and East South Central—the picture is quite bleak. Losses are persistent and deep, totaling 20 to 30 percent by 2029.

While not all locations within a division must follow identical paths, local projections mapped in figure 5.4 show considerable homogeneity within most census divisions. For instance, the HEDI anticipates two-year enrollment decreases of more than 15 percent in 16 of 24 locations in the four divisions making up the northeast quadrant of the country. Enrollments in the remaining eight locations within these divisions are expected to fall by no less than 6 percent. In other words, while not all locations are equal, the range in this part of the country is from bad to worse. Similarly, we anticipate robust growth throughout the northern half of the Mountain West. The only "outlier" is Denver, which can nevertheless expect 7 percent growth in two-year enrollments. While the short distance between students' high schools and attended two-year institutions suggests that relevant markets are smaller than can be studied with the available data, the spatial correlation evident in figure 5.4 suggests that two-year institutions drawing from only a portion of a given metropolitan area or nonurban portion of states are likely to experience futures similar to that city or state.

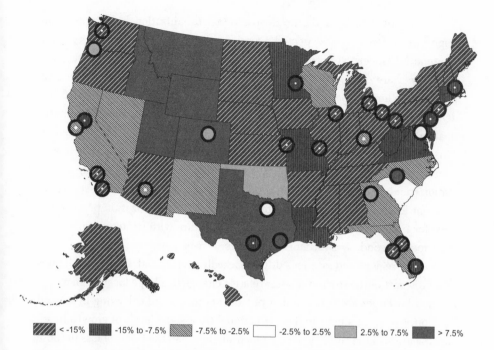

| ⧄⧄ < -15% | ▓▓ -15% to -7.5% | ▨▨ -7.5% to -2.5% | ☐ -2.5% to 2.5% | ▨ 2.5% to 7.5% | ■ > 7.5% |

Figure 5.4. Forecasted rate of growth in students who will attend two-year institutions, 2012 to 2029

Interestingly, just as in the college-aged population as a whole, the share of two-year college demand derived from metropolitan areas is expected to remain all but constant, rising from 50.7 percent in 2012 to 51 percent in 2029. While this is similar to the urbanization trend anticipated in the demand for college in general, the explanation is quite different. In the case of broad college demand, the extremely high any-college attendance rate almost dictates that urbanization patterns among the general college-going population follow those found in the population as a whole. By contrast, only one-third of students in the ELS attended a two-year institution in the first two years following high school completion. As a distinct minority of the population, it would be possible to find two-year attendance patterns that deviate from those in the population at large. Thus it is notable that while two-year college demand is a percentage point less urban than the college-going population at large, this gap is expected to remain unchanged in coming years, such that the degree of urbanness in the two-year college student population remains constant.

This relative stasis in the level of national urbanization hides potentially important differences in expected experiences across census divisions. In the Mountain, East North Central, and New England divisions, the HEDI anticipates a smaller share of students originating in metropolitan areas (down modestly between 0.2 and 0.6 percentage points). At the same time, the share of such students in the Middle Atlantic is expected to grow by 2.8 points. The urban shares in all other divisions are expected to grow by no more than one percentage point. This variation in expected changes to urbanization among two-year students stands in contrast with the homogeneity found in chapter 4 concerning urbanization trends among the college-bound in general. As with the forecasts for enrollment levels, the different expected experiences of urbanization point to the need for two-year institutions to approach the future with strategies tailored to their specific conditions rather than to national averages.

Because regions and locations differ markedly in size, analysis of growth rates tells only part of the story; a modest relative change in a large location may represent a far larger absolute number of students than a radical swing in a small location. Not surprisingly, in light of national trends, the levels of growth in advancing areas of the country will be much smaller than the levels of loss in those areas that are shrinking. On a divisional level, losses are an order of magnitude larger than gains. (Sadly, this is a literal use of the phrase *order of magnitude.*) The Pacific and East North Central anticipate particularly large reductions of approximately 40,000 two-year students each. But even in the East South Central and Middle Atlantic (down about 25,000 students each) and West North Central and South Atlantic (off more than 10,000 students each), the losses will be large. By contrast, the only growing divisions—the Mountain and West South Central— expect fewer than 5,000 additional students. At the local level, the magnitudes of loss in areas of greatest contraction, such as Los Angeles, New York City, and Tennessee, are about four times the size of gains in the areas of greatest growth— Houston, rural Texas, and Utah. Once again, the fact that the ratio of losses to gains is larger at the divisional than at the local level reflects the strong spatial correlation in growth prospects among localities within the same division, a pattern that is visible in figure 5.4.

Even though census divisions currently differ markedly in their population distributions across racial/ethnic groups, and even though the divisions expect to experience divergent paths in the numbers of two-year college students over the next 15 years, the anticipated direction and degree of change in the shares of racial/ethnic population subgroups is remarkably uniform throughout the country. With only three exceptions, projected changes in the share of each race/ethnicity category within each division fall within two points of those for the country as a whole. In New England, the division's disproportionately white two-year college population will begin to look more like the rest of the nation. The share of non-Hispanic white students will fall by 10 percentage points, about two-thirds faster than the rate of change expected for the country as a whole. Interestingly, this reduction in non-Hispanic whites is accompanied by an increase in the non-Hispanic black share, even as that group falls in the national distribution. This, too, will bring New England more in line with the rest of the country. The South Atlantic similarly anticipates reversion to the national mean, with an unusually large reduction (six percentage points) in the share of two-year students identifying as non-Hispanic blacks. Finally, the Mountain West, currently tilted toward Hispanic students, expects slower than average growth in the share of this group. On the whole, institutions in all divisions will face progressively more similar challenges in meeting the needs of an increasingly Hispanic student body.

The HEDI also predicts that all areas will share a common trend in the degree of parental attachment to higher education. Every division anticipates an increase in the share of two-year students drawn from families in which both parents hold a bachelor's degree. While this general trend is seen in each division, two nuanced differences are worth calling out. First, in the South Central, the anticipated trend is slightly muted: the HEDI forecasts that the share of students from two-baccalaureate homes will rise by five percentage points as compared to a seven-point rise nationwide. At the same time, in the Middle Atlantic (and New England, to a lesser degree), the shift away from students with low parental education background will be faster than the national average: the share of "no-BA" two-year students in the Middle Atlantic will fall by 10 percentage points, two-thirds more than in the country as a whole.

These cases exemplify a general pattern: census divisions that currently draw a larger share of their two-year students from highly educated families will see the largest shift toward stronger parental education backgrounds. Unlike the case of the racial/ethnic distribution where forecasts point to greater homogeneity across census divisions, along the dimension of parental connection to higher education the HEDI anticipates increasing divergence in two-year college experiences over the next 15 years. To quantify this difference, the variance across census divisions in the share of non-Hispanic white students is projected to fall by 10 percent, while the variance in the share of first-generation students is projected to double.[3] This suggests that while the two-year sector may be able to compare notes nationally on new strategies for teaching effectively for an increasingly Hispanic student body, responses to changes in family educational background may need to be somewhat more regional.

The Challenges Ahead

The primary challenge for the two-year sector in the next 15 years is clear: dramatically reduced enrollments. Indeed, the expected rate of contraction in two-year enrollments is almost 20 percent faster than for college enrollments in general. With the exception of the Mountain and East South Central census divisions, which anticipate very modest growth, losses in demand will be found throughout the country. In four census divisions, projected losses exceed 15 percent. The Pacific and East South Central are notable in that the expected rate of loss in two-year students exceeds that for college enrollments in general by five or more percentage points. In sum, two-year colleges in much of the country are expected to be exaggerated exemplars of the dreary demographics called out in the headlines.

Compounding enrollment challenges, the racial/ethnic makeup of two-year students is anticipated to shift to a greater degree than in the college-aged population more generally. Indeed, while the HEDI anticipates that enrollments among non-Hispanic whites and non-Hispanic blacks will plummet by 20 and 30 percent, respectively, the number of Hispanic students is expected to grow by 10 percent. Combined, these forces will increase Hispanic shares by six points. These patterns will be experienced throughout the country: All nine divisions project fewer non-Hispanic white students in 2029 than in 2012, and eight of the nine anticipate more Hispanics. The lone exception to the latter rule is the Pacific, which already serves a student body in which Hispanics make up a plurality and which is home to 40 percent of all Hispanic two-year enrollments in 2012. In that context, the small (4 percent) reduction in Hispanic demand is a footnote. Thus two-year institutions everywhere must anticipate serving more minority students while likely grappling with budget pressures related to steep enrollment cuts everywhere outside the Mountain and East South Central divisions. In total, the two-year landscape generally conforms to the popular narrative read in the headlines.

Ideas for how institutions may respond to these challenges are discussed in chapter 8. But before taking up those questions, the projections described above raise another interesting point: if projected demand for two-year colleges is expected to contract by more than the college-aged population as a whole, then some or all subgroups of the four-year sector must be expected to outperform the predictions for college-going in general. Similarly, if two-year schools expect to experience an exaggerated shift toward Hispanic students, then some or all four-year schools must anticipate a muted move in this direction. The next chapters look more carefully at the market for four-year education and find pockets of the industry that will look nothing like the picture painted by the dominant narrative.

Chapter Six

Demand for Four-Year Institutions

W e now turn to the use of the Higher Education Demand Index at four-year colleges and universities, the sector that has dramatically grown during the second half of the twentieth century and is, indeed, what much of the population thinks of as simply "college." The last 75 years were golden years for this sector of higher education. The percentage of individuals ages 25 to 29 who hold a bachelor's degree has increased from just more than 5 percent in 1940 to more than 35 percent in 2016 (NCES 2016, table 104.20). During the same period, the high school degree was transformed from a distinguishing achievement into something quite common; approximately 90 percent of individuals in their late 20s held a diploma by 1990, up from just 40 percent in 1940. Coincident with rising rates of educational uptake, the population of young people almost doubled. The ultimate effect of these two forces has been a 10-fold increase in the number of persons in their late 20s who hold a bachelor's degree.[1] Yet, despite this impressive increase in the supply of educated workers, the return to a college degree has increased by 60 percent since 1980 (Goldin and Katz 2008). While HEDI forecasts suggest new challenges for four-year schools, the picture is still notably stronger than what we just saw for two-year colleges, and for many four-year schools the future remains quite promising.

National Forecasts

The HEDI forecasts presented in figure 6.1 suggest that the four-year sector will experience modest enrollment increases over the next decade before a sig-

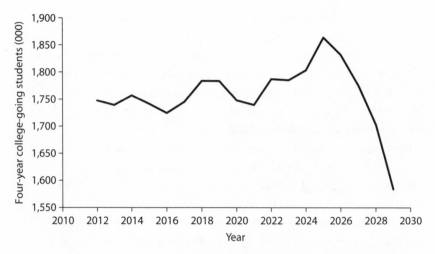

Figure 6.1. Forecasted number of four-year college-going students, by year of high school graduation

nificant contraction begins in the mid-2020s. Between now and 2023, the number of students attending a four-year institution in the two years following high school graduation is expected to fall within 2 percent of enrollment levels today. Following this period of stability, the HEDI shows a 7 percent rise through the year 2025 before the weight of the current birth dearth reduces enrollment more than 15 percent in the latter half of the 2020s. In just four years, at the end of the forecast horizon, the four-year sector stands to lose almost 280,000 students. Accounting for both the brief increase and the subsequent decline, the model predicts approximately 150,000 (or 10 percent) fewer students in 2029 than today, a contraction only modestly smaller than that predicted for college-going in general. Obviously, this anticipated reversal is small compared to the decades-long trend of growth over the past century. To put it in context, a 10 percent drop in college-going would mean that only 4.5 million, rather than 5 million, persons in their late 20s will possess a bachelor's degree by the mid-2030s. This total would still exceed the number of bachelor's recipients in every year before 1980. So, the HEDI forecasts in no way signal the end of the four-year degree. Still, after 60 years of steady growth in demand, the future will present significant challenges for many institutions.

While the predicted rise and fall in the aggregate number of students who attend four-year institutions has significant implications for many national policy questions, individual institutions may rightly wonder whether the demand for their institutions will follow a similar path. Chapters 1 and 2 provide evidence for changing demographics that may lead to greater demand for some types of four-year institutions, even as others struggle to succeed in ever-shrinking recruitment pools. To explore this possibility, the HEDI generates separate demand forecasts for three groups by institution rank: those ranked by *US News & World Report* among the top 50 national colleges and universities, those ranked 51 to 100 in the same list, and those ranked outside the top 100 schools.[2]

The geographic markets for institutions in these three subsets of the four-year sector vary dramatically in size. We can see this by measuring the median distance between a student's high school and an attended college in the 2002 Education Longitudinal Study.[3] Among the subset of students who attended an institution ranked outside the top 100 schools, half traveled 60 miles or less to college. (The interquartile range lies between 15 and 155 miles.) While this distance is four times that for two-year colleges attended, the relatively short travel distance suggests that the majority of students attending such institutions are likely to hail from the same census division. For this reason, institutions outside the top 100 will be referred to as *regional* four-year institutions in the analysis that follows.

By contrast, institutions ranked among the top 100 have a more national recruitment pool. The median student attending a school ranked 51 through 100 traveled 110 miles from their high school (with an interquartile range between 50 and 220 miles). At top-50 schools, the median distance traveled is even larger: 175 miles (with an interquartile range between 65 and 465). While institutions in the former group clearly retain regional flavors, at least one-quarter of their students move more than 220 miles to attend college. Reflecting this reality, in subsequent discussions these schools will be called *national* colleges and universities. The highest-ranked institution group clearly attracts a national applicant pool. (Note that the average student at such schools travels farther than the 75th-percentile student attending an institution ranked outside the top 100.) These schools will be referred to as *elite* colleges and universities.[4]

Using these definitions, figure 6.2 plots distinct HEDI demand forecasts for regional (panel a), national (panel b), and elite colleges and universities (panel c). The results point to a distinctly different future for four-year schools of different types. In the next 10 years, growth is expected to be much stronger among top-ranked institutions (close to 25 percent) than for regional schools (6 percent). Then, around 2025, all three subgroups show clear effects of the birth dearth with an acute, negative change in trend. However, the relative size of the resulting drop is smaller among higher-ranked institutions. In fact, the reversal among

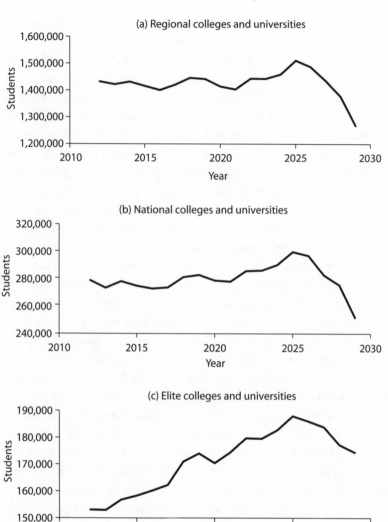

Figure 6.2. Forecasted number of four-year college-going students, by institution type and year of high school graduation

elite schools (9 percent) is about half that anticipated for institutions outside the top 100 (17 percent). Because demand prospects differ substantially both in the initial period of growth and during the birth-dearth contraction, the net effect is a distinct advantage for elite institutions (up almost 15 percent) relative to regional colleges and universities (down by nearly an equal degree), with national schools breaking even until the final year of the forecast, when demand takes a decidedly negative dip to end down 10 percent.

On the surface, figure 6.2 might seem to suggest that only the highest-ranked schools will navigate the effects of the birth dearth without serious budgetary pressures. However, careful interpretation of the forecasts provides reason for optimism among second-tier institutions as well. The HEDI predicts the number of future students who possess characteristics associated with college attendance today. Such students will only have the chance to attend a particular college if admitted. That outcome depends on institutions' admissions policies as much as on students' characteristics. So, the trends in figure 6.2 represent potential demand rather than actual attendance. To understand the meaning of the forecasts for national schools, we must ask whether elite schools will increase enrollments to admit all students with a demographic profile similar to their students today. That seems unlikely, especially at residential institutions, where enrollment changes require expensive building projects. The anticipated pattern of future demand—a substantial rise followed by significant reversal—makes such capital investments risky in the long run. While enrollments at such institutions may continue the upward drift of recent years, it seems unlikely that elite schools will expand sufficiently to meet all of the student demand predicted by the model.

This creates the potential for students to "trickle down" from one institution group to the next. The number of students with characteristics consistent with attending an elite institution is predicted to grow by roughly 20,000 by 2029. This increase is more than three-quarters of the predicted loss in national college and university enrollments. If top-ranked schools do not grow by 15 percent to meet fully the increase in their demand, significant relief may be available for second-tier institutions. For example, if elite schools grow no more than 5 percent in the next 15 years, then the growth in top-tier students unable to get into those schools would offset more than half the expected reduction in demand for national institutions.

Of course, while this observation provides comfort for second-tier institutions, it offers no relief to regional four-year institutions. The growth in demand at the top is simply too small to overcome the substantial losses expected by colleges and universities outside the top 100. Indeed, the same arguments suggest the contraction at regional schools may be worse than represented in figure 6.2. Faced with lagging enrollments by the very end of the 2020s, national schools may change recruitment and admissions practices to attract students who in the past have attended regional institutions. While this could marginally deepen enrollment reductions at regional schools, the scale of national institutions is too small for this student substitution to have a meaningful impact on the picture painted earlier. Even in the most pessimistic case, in which national schools manage to recover 100 percent of their 27,000 lost students by drawing new enrollments out of regional schools, the ultimate loss at regional schools would increase only from 11 percent to 13 percent. Such recruitment competition may be critical to individual institutions, but it doesn't create a new reality for the industry as a whole.

Local Forecasts

While aggregate predictions look hopeful for elite and, to a lesser degree, national schools, even within these groups the geographic distribution of students will shift across geography in ways that may call for new recruitment strategies. Of course, it isn't as simple as moving recruiters into areas of projected growth. The current and future recruiting strategies of competitors will also be important determinants of the best response to the coming demographic change. If Institution A knows that Institution B, against whom A fares poorly in head-to-head competition, is expanding recruitment in a high-growth area, A may opt to pursue students in an area with slightly poorer growth prospects to avoid wasting recruitment dollars in a futile competition. However, even acknowledging these kinds of complications in the design of optimal admissions office strategies, it is clear that the first step in any successful strategy involves figuring out where the growth is likely to occur.

The divisional variation in HEDI's forecasts for demand for regional four-year institutions is stark.[5] The northeast quadrant of the country expects a steady, modest decline until the mid-2020s, when the birth dearth will lead to an acceleration in the rate of contraction. The net losses are substantial: down approximately 20 percent in the Middle Atlantic and 25 percent in both the East North Central and New England. That such changes are predicted in such a short time span suggests painful changes ahead for the many institutions in this part of the country. By contrast, for the next decade the Pacific, Mountain, and South Atlantic divisions expect gains of 10 percent while the West South Central grows by more than 20 percent. Despite these substantial growth rates, the subsequent contraction caused by the birth dearth more than offsets this growth, leaving all but the Pacific division in the red—and in that division, growth will fall well short of 1 percent. So, even regional four-year institutions in areas expecting mid-term growth should likely avoid making long-term commitments if

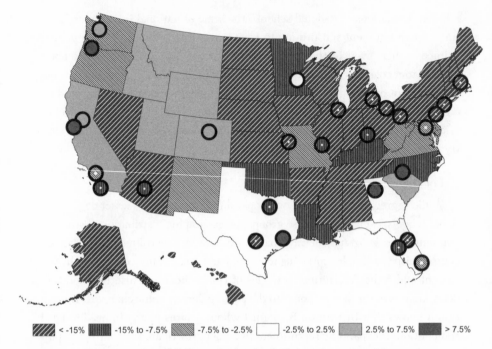

Figure 6.3. Forecasted growth in students who will attend a regional four-year institution, 2012 to 2029

they expand operations to reach the growing student population over the next decade.

The same data are studied on a more granular level in figure 6.3, which maps expected growth in metropolitan areas and nonmetropolitan portions of states. The picture bears a grim resemblance to the forecast maps in chapter 4, which report changes to population and postsecondary schooling demand. With the exceptions of Atlanta, South Carolina (including Charlotte), and Houston, the model predicts that over the next 15 years, substantially fewer students from areas east of the Rockies will attend regional colleges and universities. The Midwest and Northeast, markets currently accounting for almost half of the regional higher education market, appear particularly weak, with all but three submarkets in these regions projected to contract by 15 percent or more. What little growth there may be is driven by expansions in concentrated parts of California and the sparsely populated Mountain West.

While it may not be possible to paint a scarier picture than that in figure 6.3, we can give it a go by recasting these growth rates into changes in absolute numbers of students. The model predicts fewer students from eight of the nine census divisions. In fact, with the exception of the Pacific, which expects to expand by only 1,000 students, a closer examination of divisional "bright spots" in the South and West simply shows losses measured in the thousands, rather than in tens of thousands. Losses are particularly sharp in the East North Central and Middle Atlantic, two of the three largest divisions in terms of regional college and university attendance, where the HEDI forecasts contractions of approximately 50,000 students each. New England and the West North Central will each add around 15,000 to the total losses.

On the level of states and metropolitan areas, the forecasts follow similar geographic patterns. The areas of largest loss are concentrated in the Northeast and Midwest: New York City (down 20,000), nonmetropolitan New York (down 10,000), Chicago (down 10,000), Boston (down 9,000), and Detroit (down 8,000). Areas of largest absolute gain congregate in Texas and the west: Houston, Atlanta, San Francisco, and Portland. The absolute magnitudes of gains and losses reiterate the broader national story: the losses found among the largest losers are almost four times as large as the expansions expected among the largest winners.

If anything, the HEDI's predictions for regional four-year institutions are more negative than the dominant narrative put forth by outlets such as the *Chronicle of Higher Education*. The population growth in the Southwest heralded by such headlines is concentrated in populations that aren't likely to attend a regional four-year school. As seen in chapter 5, the HEDI predicts growth in the number of such students attending two-year schools. And, as the following shows, growth forecasts in the Southwest are strong for national and elite institutions. If regional four-year schools in the Southwest are going to tap into the benefits of population growth in the Southwest, then they will need to find new recruitment strategies to draw students whose demographic markers suggest they are bound for other parts of the higher education market.

The overall picture is substantially better for institutions ranked among the top 100 colleges and universities. Figures 6.4 and 6.5 present similar data for national and elite institutions. For national institutions (ranks 51 through 100), the country offers substantially more growth opportunities. While regional four-year institutions expect contraction in eight of nine census divisions, national schools expect strong growth in the Pacific and Mountain divisions, up 9 percent and 16 percent, respectively, while the West South Central and South Atlantic hold more or less even. Still, the outlook for the Northeast and Midwest—the

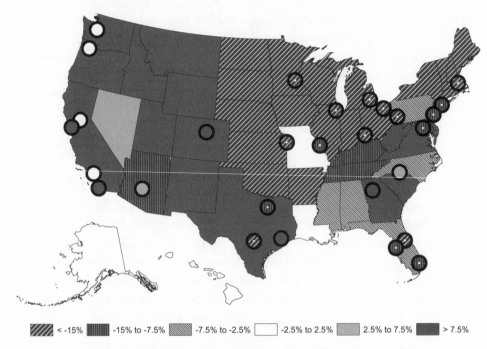

Figure 6.4. Forecasted rate of growth in students who will attend national four-year institutions, 2012 to 2029

regions of origin for approximately half of all students attending such schools—remains disturbingly negative, with rates of decline in excess of 15 percent in total and by more than one-quarter in the East North Central and New England.

When looked at by state and metropolitan area, there are clear opportunities. Even as regional schools expect only a few positive spots in a sea of red, for second-tier institutions nearly the entire West and parts of the Southeast open up in promise of robust demand growth between 2012 and 2029. Still, losses in the Midwest and Northeast are troublingly widespread: with the exception of nonmetropolitan Missouri, every single locale within these regions foresees significant contraction. Still, despite tough projections for the northeast quadrant of the country, the picture is undoubtedly stronger for national than for regional institutions. For example, among areas of largest gain and loss, the magnitudes of losses are only twice those of gains. So, while losses of more than 2,500 students each in Boston, Chicago, and New York City will create challenges, gains of 2,000 students in Houston and 1,000 more each in Atlanta and nonmetropolitan California offer offsetting opportunities. National schools that can shade their recruitment activities toward the Southeast and West may find students to replace losses in their more traditional prospective student pools.

Moving even further up the college and university rankings, HEDI analysis of demand for elite institutions provides an almost sanguine picture (figure 6.5). Positive growth is predicted for seven of the nine census divisions, 65 percent of metropolitan areas and 70 percent of nonmetropolitan portions of states. However, traditional recruiting regions remain the areas of greatest challenge: the East North Central and New England divisions expect to lose about 2,500 and 1,500 students, respectively—losses of 10 percent or more. However, gains in the West North Central and Middle Atlantic essentially offset these contractions so that the model forecasts little net change in either the Midwest or Northeast regions as a whole. Gains in the Mountain and West South Central could be astounding, as elite students double and triple (up 5,000 and 10,000, respectively) in these divisions. At the level of the state or metropolitan area, the areas of largest expected loss continue to be in traditional recruitment markets including Boston, Philadelphia, nonmetropolitan Michigan, and combined states of Maine,

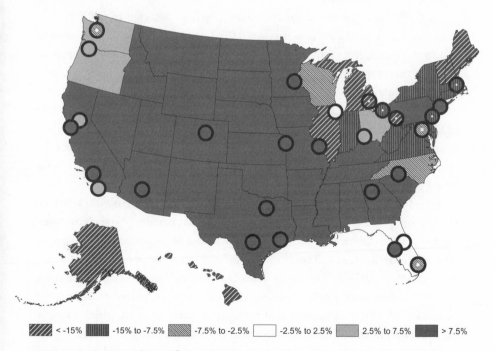

< -15%   -15% to -7.5%   -7.5% to -2.5%   -2.5% to 2.5%   2.5% to 7.5%   > 7.5%

Figure 6.5. Forecasted rate of growth in students who will attend an elite national four-year institution, 2012 to 2029

New Hampshire, and Vermont. However, the losses will be much smaller—only 600 or 700 students—than the largest gains posted in areas such as nonmetropolitan Texas (up 3,500), Los Angeles (up 1,900), or Dallas and Houston (up more than 1,700 each). Moreover, the numerically important New York City market is predicted to be among the areas of largest growth, up by 1,800 elite students, or 10 percent. In total, most top-tier institutions could navigate the coming demographic shifts with very modest changes in recruitment strategies.

Of course, what is possible may not be advisable. While many elite institutions may be able to fill their classes without substantially altering the geographic makeups of their campuses, the HEDI suggests real opportunities for institutions that exhibit flexibility and adaptability. Specifically, a corridor running just west of the Mississippi River from Minnesota to Texas anticipates widespread, expansive growth. Every metropolitan area and nonmetropolitan portion of a state in this central column of the country foresees growth of at least 20 percent. These gains will be impressive in absolute terms as well: over the next 15 years, the model predicts twice as many students—an increase of more than 10,000—in the corridor as a whole.

Similarly, with the exception of Seattle, which is projected to fall a modest 4 percent, the West Coast shows substantial and widespread growth. Even though the aggregate expected growth rate in this area rises to only 15 percent, because the area currently contributes a large number of elite-bound students, the predicted absolute change in this region still tops 4,700. This increase accounts for 22 percent of the market growth for the entire country. So, it may be possible (and comfortable) for many top-tier institutions to continue drawing students from the same prospective student pools, but those that are able to adapt recruitment strategies to reach the new student populations will be able to draw on a larger pool, and so presumably enroll stronger students.

Even though projections for demand at elite institutions are clearly stronger than those for other institution types, the northeast portion of the country remains an important weak spot. Elites that attract a disproportionate number of students from this area will certainly feel pressure over the next 15 years. For example, approximately 40 percent of Bates College and Bowdoin College students are drawn from New England, where elite demand is expected to fall nearly 15 percent. Another 25 percent hail from the Middle Atlantic, which expects only modest growth. While such schools are unlikely to struggle to fill their incoming classes, meaningful changes to recruitment strategies will be needed to avoid losing ground in terms of student quality to peers who are expected to choose from a quickly growing pool.

While aggregate gains among elite institutions nearly offset losses in the second tier (recall figure 6.2), a regional analysis suggests second-tier institutions may need to adjust recruitment strategies if they want to benefit from the potential "trickle down." Because national and elite schools draw from similar populations, their regional growth patterns are strongly correlated. As a result, growth among top-tier students rarely offsets losses in the second tier in a given division. For example, in the East North Central, where the second tier expects to see 13,000 fewer students, top-tier schools expect demand to fall by 2,500 students. Similarly, in the Middle Atlantic and New England divisions, the second tier anticipates losing 10,000 students, while the demand for top schools falls by another 500. To the extent that elite schools find it difficult to alter regional recruitment strategies, some of these top institutions may respond to contracting prospective student pools by relaxing admission standards to make the most of the shrinking populations in long-standing recruitment areas. This will only compound contraction experienced by second-tier institutions hunting for students in these same, down markets.

Even in divisions or regions in which we expect little change in the sum of national and elite students, we should not assume second-tier institutions will find recruiting to be easy. For example, the number of students available to top-50-ranked institutions in New York City is expected rise by 10 percent. This may at first sound like a place where second-tier schools might benefit from "trickle down"; however, if demographic changes pressure elite institutions to adjust recruitment strategies, New York City (an already heavily recruited market) might be one of the first places they will look to make up for losses elsewhere. Therefore, it seems relatively unlikely that elite students in New York City will trickle down to national institutions. In total, if elite schools respond to shifting student populations, second-tier schools will need to be nimble, responding to recruitment strategies among top-tier schools and their peers, to realize the hope of benefiting from areas of excess growth in elite students. And if elite schools do not alter recruitment in light of changing student populations, successful second-tier schools will require even greater flexibility to capitalize on new populations of prospective students. Chapter 8 offers a more detailed description of what this might look like.

The Changing Face of the Four-Year Student Body

If you walk into a student center in 2030, will you hear and see a student body that requires different educational approaches and academic support than what is available today? In other words, will the demographic makeup of four-year-college students be noticeably different in 15 years? Figure 6.6 plots current and forecasted geographic distributions of students by institution type. Relative to the 18-year-old population, four-year institutions as a whole currently draw disproportionately fewer students from the West and South, and more from the Midwest and Northeast. Elite institutions differ somewhat from others, drawing substantially larger shares of their students from both coasts. In the broad category of all four-year institutions, expected geographic changes between now and 2029 are relatively modest. The share of four-year-college-going students from any given census region is expected to change by no more than three percentage points. Such changes may be recognized in institutional research offices, but they are not likely to be palpable in the student center. If elite schools admit students in proportion to the evolving geographic distribution of students in their pool, changes may be slightly more noticeable at these top colleges and universities. Among students with demographic characteristics predictive of attending top-50 schools, the share from the South Central region is forecasted to double at

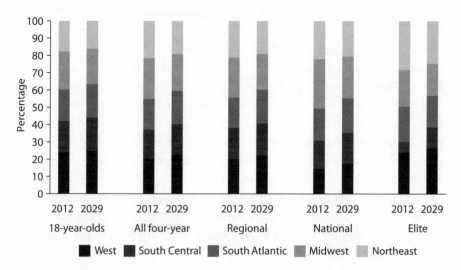

Figure 6.6. Forecasted geographic distribution of students attending four-year institutions, 2012 and 2029

the expense of market share drawn from the Midwest and East Coast. Drilling deeper into the data, the HEDI predicts that the share of elite students drawn from the East North Central and New England divisions will fall by 5.4 percentage points (a reduction of more than 20 percent). Despite their modest absolute magnitudes, this adjustment may indeed be tangible on these elite campuses (though perhaps not given offsetting gains in other Midwest and Northeast divisions).

Instead of dividing geography into contiguous regions, we might be interested in distinguishing between demand from metropolitan versus nonmetropolitan areas. The HEDI predicts a notably stronger trend toward urban centers in the demand for regional four-year schools than for college-going in general. Between 2012 and 2029, the national share of regional four-year students originating in metropolitan areas is expected to increase by 1.4 percentage points. While each division anticipates greater urbanization in 2029 than today, the divisions can be divided into two distinct groups. Little change (less than 0.5 percentage points) is expected in the Pacific, Mountain, East South Central, and South Atlantic. By contrast, in Texas and the northeast quadrant of the county the urban share is expected to rise by between 1.5 and 2.0 points. While greater than that found in the broad college-going population, the cross-divisional range of predicted urbanization rates is smaller in the case of regional four-year-college students than for two-year-college students. As a result, this largest group of four-year colleges might find a greater degree of similarity in the challenges they face around increasing urbanness of student populations (though the shifts are admittedly small in all cases).

A very different picture emerges in the demand for national and elite institutions. First, unlike in the cases of the college-aged population and the demands for two-year and regional four-year institutions, the HEDI predicts decreased urbanization among students at top-50 institutions. Second-tier institutions can expect no change in the share of students drawn from metropolitan areas, which stands at 56.2 percent for 2012, while elite schools anticipate a reversal of national trends as the urban share drops almost two points, from 64.2 to 62.3 percent. While all of the forecasted changes in urbanization among four-year student groups are likely too small to warrant significant changes to campus programming, it is notable that the HEDI predicts greater homogeneity across institution types in the future, as the highly urbanized elite student bodies are expected to become less distinct in this dimension in coming years.

Many have presumed that rising minority populations in the country will inevitably translate into more or less proportional changes in enrollment at all types of colleges. For example, in a 2013 *Chronicle of Higher Education* story, Hoover (2013b) uses high school graduation forecasts to predict changing demographics among college students. Having seen different attendance rates across race/ethnicity groups, we know that a full analysis requires far more than high school graduate head counts. Figure 6.7 presents HEDI forecasts of the racial/ethnic makeup of four-year-college-going students. The share of non-Hispanic whites is expected to fall by a bit more than five percentage points in most categories of four-year institutions—a shift that matches the expected change in the population of 18-year-olds (leftmost set of columns in the figure). Despite this congruency in expected trends for the non-Hispanic white share, four-year colleges should expect shifts in racial/ethnic distributions that differ from the population at large. Specifically, in the population as a whole, the largest expected growth in population share is found among Hispanics, who will gain five percentage points. By contrast, on four-year campuses the increased representation of Hispanics will be somewhat muted, while the HEDI predicts relatively more growth in the representation of Asian Americans.

As with geographic change, the absolute magnitudes of change are quite small. It seems unlikely that many will immediately discern the difference between campuses that are 61 percent non-Hispanic white (today, at all four-year institu-

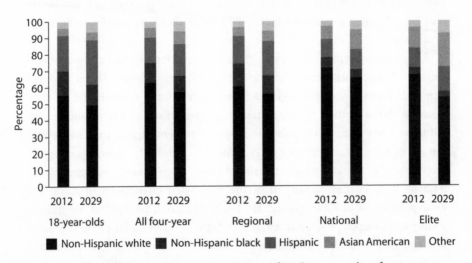

Figure 6.7. Forecasted race/ethnicity distribution of students attending four-year institutions, 2012 and 2029

tions) and those that are 56 percent non-Hispanic white (predicted for all four-year institutions in 2029). However, also as in the case of geographic change, elite institutions will experience stronger demographic change if their admissions follow the available pool of students. Among top-50-ranked institutions, the share of non-Hispanic white students is predicted to fall by 14 percentage points (or more than 20 percent). However, at these schools, while the Hispanic share will grow by three points, the great contributor to racial/ethnic diversification will be an outsized eight-percentage-point increase in the share of Asian American students—an increase in share of more than 60 percent. Second-tier national institutions are predicted to follow a slightly less dramatic version of the elite institutions' path. In all, changes to college distributions across race/ethnicity are coming to institutions of all types, but at some it won't appear as "a surge of Hispanic" students, as suggested by Hoover (2013b).

Of course, choices by admissions departments could easily mitigate or amplify these changes. In particular, the strong growth in demand for elite schools could buy them the ability to ignore population trends in favor of maintaining the status quo. It is easy to imagine some admissions officers preferring this more conservative strategy over expanding recruitment into untested markets. In addition, top institutions may feel pressure to preserve the traditional "feel" of their campuses by lagging behind demographic trends. If for these or other reasons elites choose not to expand enrollments, and, particularly, if they fill their seats with only modest changes to recruitment strategies, students who trickle down to second-tier institutions would disproportionately identify as Asian American and, to a lesser degree, Hispanic. As a result, we could see substantially greater diversification among second-tier schools than what is suggested by figure 6.7.

These predictions for the shares of racial/ethnic groups are intertwined with forecasts of the distribution across parental education presented in figure 6.8. In the coming decades, the HEDI predicts greater shares of college-going students from households with high parent educational attainment. In all but the elite institutions, the share of first-generation students (defined as students not living with a parent who holds a bachelor's degree) will fall by more than five percentage points, an amount slightly greater than the drop anticipated in the full population of 18-year-olds. The share of students drawn from homes with only one parental bachelor's will also drop—by four percentage points at regional four-year institutions and by more than twice that amount at institutions ranked within the top 100 colleges and universities. As

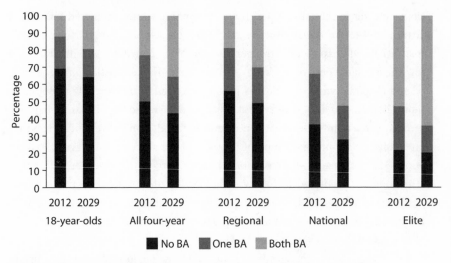

Figure 6.8. Forecasted parental education distribution of students attending four-year institutions, 2012 and 2029

a result, the share of students from homes with two bachelor's degrees will increase by more than 10 percentage points in all three institutional tiers. For regional schools, this will represent a 60 percent increase in the population share of students whose parents have strong educational connections. At national and elite schools, the increase in share represents more modest increases of roughly 20 percent because such institutions' student bodies already skew toward populations with strong parent education. Unlike forecasted changes to geographic and race/ethnicity distributions, movements of this size may easily be "felt" on campus.

Because higher education institutions value diversity in family background, admissions offices may attempt to push against this trend, targeting populations with weaker family attachments to higher education. As discussed previously, this kind of admissions choice seems particularly plausible at elite institutions, whose endowments and excess future demand give them an additional degree of choice. If these schools are successful in maintaining their current parent education distributions, then any trickle down to other national institutions will be tilted toward students with deeper family educational experience. That would, in turn, create a shift in the parent education distribution at second-tier schools that is even greater than that presented in figure 6.8.

The Challenges Ahead

With more than 40 percent of all young people attending a four-year institution at some point in the first two years following high school graduation, it is difficult for major population changes to affect the whole while leaving this subgroup unchanged. As a result, the HEDI predicts a decade of modest growth in four-year attendance followed by a sharp contraction as the current birth-dearth generation reaches college-going age. However, this aggregate story obscures important differences by geography and institution type.

Due to their regional recruitment markets, schools ranked outside the top 100 colleges and universities should expect very different trends, depending on location. (In this way, their futures will be similar to two-year schools.) In particular, the western half of the country along with the South Atlantic division expect little gain or loss. By contrast, in eastern census divisions the number of students enrolled in regional four-year institutions is expected to fall by 20 percent or more. Because students served by these institutions rarely travel more than 150 miles for college, it is unlikely that these differences will be smoothed over by greater student mobility. Thus regional institutions will have very distinct experiences. Interestingly, while much has been made of coming changes in racial/ethnic composition, regional institutions can anticipate less change in this dimension than in higher education in general. Moreover, increases in educational acquisition in the past foreshadow a reduction in first-generation students at such schools. As a result, while regional schools as a group will face intense enrollment pressure, changes in the composition of their student bodies should not complicate their futures as much as at other institution types.

By contrast, elite schools expect healthy demand increases driven by rising levels of parent education and an increasing Asian American population with strong connections to higher education. Only the Northeast expects contraction in demand in this subsector; the rest of the country predicts strong growth. Students' willingness to travel to such institutions minimizes the importance of even this exception. The biggest enrollment threat to these colleges and universities will be overexpansion between now and 2025, when the effects of the birth dearth kick in. While most of these top schools will likely avoid problems due to enrollment declines, demographic change will still pose challenges. In both race and geography, recruitment pools of elite institutions will experience larger shifts than at other four-year schools. Even though it will often be possible to maintain enrollment levels without changing recruitment strategies (and possibly making related changes to student support services), flexibility and a willingness to look in new markets may yield better cohorts of incoming classes with more-representative family backgrounds. While leaders at these institutions will undoubtedly feel pressure to make the most of the pool they are given, when compared to the stresses at other colleges and universities that may be fighting for survival, such recruitment challenges are relatively pleasant to consider.

The greatest uncertainty will likely be experienced by second-tier national colleges and universities. "Status quo" strategies are unlikely to succeed, as the number of second-tier students is expected to fall in large portions of the country. Rising demand for elite schools will likely outstrip supply, providing relief for some second-tier schools. But how exactly should national institutions alter recruitment strategies to take best advantage of the growing numbers of top students who can't all be accepted at top schools? Because growing demand for elite schools makes for a range of successful paths for top colleges and universities, it isn't possible to answer this question precisely. What is clear is that nimbleness will be a notable characteristic of successful second-tier schools. Chapter 8 provides more detail about what that may look like.

But before considering institutional changes in response to demand fluctuations, an implicit assumption must be articulated and explored. In chapters 4 through 6, the focus has been on students numbers. While the success of higher education institutions clearly depends on there being "enough" students, it is equally clear that this is not sufficient. High-cost private institutions in particular require full-pay (or nearly full-pay) students to make their economic models work. Indeed, some students impose more costs than they are able to pay. To maintain diverse classrooms, institutions happily recruit and admit such students. But at the same time, few schools can afford to ignore the other tail of the income distribution. The next chapter considers what the HEDI has to say concerning students' ability to pay for college.

Chapter Seven

Is Anyone Paying for All of This?

While our Higher Education Demand Index predictions make it clear that the demographic outlook for the four-year sector, and especially for elite and even less prestigious national colleges and universities, may be much more optimistic than less nuanced analyses suggest, we must address another question that is foremost in most discussions: How helpful is it to have large numbers of potential students if they cannot make significant contributions toward the cost of the education they receive? Pointing to the demographic shifts ahead, Blumenstyk (2015) takes a pessimistic view: "[Demographic shifts] mean more of the students heading to college will require more in financial aid to be able to afford it—and increasing competition among colleges for the student who can afford to pay more" (81). Kolodny (1998) concurs, concluding that the increasing share of lower-income minority students among primary and secondary school students means that colleges will increasingly draw students from "poor families and even poorer school districts" (34). HEDI forecasts in previous chapters call into question the premise of these arguments, which rest on analyses of simple headcount data. Still, the broader financial question these authors raise remains: Even if the total number of college-interested students increases, will enough of them have the resources to be able to pay for the costs of higher education? This chapter takes up this question by examining HEDI forecasts for the important full-pay student subgroup.

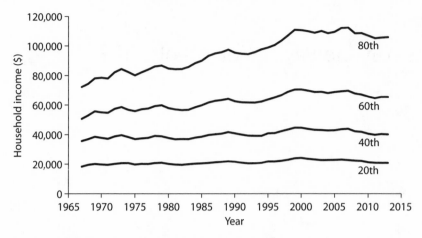

Figure 7.1. Inflation-adjusted household income (2013 dollars) 1967–2013, by percentile. *Source:* DeNavas-Walt and Proctor (2014), table A2.

With modest support from governments, selective private institutions are particularly dependent on family incomes.[1] Figure 7.1 plots the evolution of inflation-adjusted levels of household income over the past several decades at a number of points in the income distribution. From the mid-1960s through 2000, growth throughout the household income distribution supported increases in net tuition revenue.[2] Much attention has been paid to growing incomes at the top of the income distribution, and rightly so: over that four-decade span, the household income level at the 95th percentile grew 70 percent. For national institutions, these households are of particular importance because they can actually afford to pay all or most of high comprehensive fees. But in the second half of the twentieth century, income growth, while uneven, was not restricted to the wealthiest households. Upper-middle incomes (represented in figure 7.1 by the 60th- and 80th-percentile households) grew by 40 to 50 percent. Even lower-middle incomes (the 20th and 40th percentiles) made steady gains of 20 to 30 percent. In absolute terms, the gains at the bottom of the income distribution were obviously much smaller—about $6,000 at the 20th percentile as compared to $38,000 at the 80th percentile. But even so, through the end of the century, colleges recruited families with greater and greater capacity to pay tuition bills.

In response to increasing demand, colleges and universities raised fees much faster than inflation. According to the College Board (2016, table 2A), inflation-adjusted tuition and fees at public and private, two-year and four-year institutions doubled from 1981 to 2001. Of course, tuition levels vary dramatically across institution types. The increase in average tuition and fees experienced at public two-year institutions, which rose from $1,100 to $2,200, might be financed by a wide range of options, including modest increases in work while the student is in school. At $5,100, even average tuition and fees at public four-year colleges were manageable in 2001. But the same rate of increase in price tags at private four-year schools, from just less than $11,000 to more than $23,500, necessitated greater reliance on financial aid discounting—effectively charging different prices to different families. Even with growing financial aid budgets, sustained growth in incomes fueled rising net tuition revenue at private four-year institutions (College Board 2016, 21).

Since 2000, flattening income trends have led many to wonder if the decades-long model of higher education financing is broken (or is at least unsuited to a new reality). From peaks reached in that year through 2013, incomes have been stagnant or negative throughout most of the family income distribution. Incomes below the median have fallen 10 to 15 percent, while those among upper-middle-income households (the 60th to 80th percentiles) are off approximately 5 percent. Even at the 95th percentile, we have seen no growth in more than a decade. It is important to note two facts evident in figure 7.1. First, these are not solely the effects of the financial crisis of 2008. Certainly, like past downturns, the Great Recession contributed to economic weakness. But income stagnation is clearly evident long before trouble at Bear Stearns made headlines in 2007. Indeed, unexpectedly stagnant incomes in the early 2000s may have contributed to the crisis as much as the other way around. Second, the stagnation seen in incomes is unprecedented—at least in the experience of those with children nearing college age. From 1977 to 2000, 80th-percentile incomes never posted a decade-long loss. In each and every year, incomes at this point in the distribution were higher than a decade before. At the 60th percentile, only 1982 and 1983 posted negative decadal growth rates.[3] By contrast, since 2009, 60th- and 80th-percentile income levels have fallen short of those a decade before in each year.

Despite this unprecedented flattening in household incomes, tuition increases have continued with only a modest reduction in the rate of growth. While the sticker-price inflation looks impressive at private colleges and universities, the net result has been that institutions are treading water as higher discount rates offset fee increases. According to a 2016 survey of 411 private nonprofit four-year colleges and universities performed by the National Association of College and University Business Officers (NACUBO), the discount rate increased from 35 percent in 2007 to 43 percent in 2015. Given the rate of tuition increases, rising discount rates are hardly surprising, and, indeed, recent increases in discounting are a continuation of the trend begun in the 1990s. What is new is that since 2007, the average growth in net tuition revenue per full-time first-year student has only kept pace with inflation. By contrast, from 1996 through 2006, increases in net tuition revenue exceeded inflation by an average of two percentage points. These experiences make it reasonable to wonder if private institutions should abandon their long-held financial model.

The Importance of High-Income Families

Interestingly, the 1996–2006 decade of superinflationary increases in net tuition income reported by NACUBO coincided with flat incomes for the bottom four-fifths of the income distribution. This points to the relative importance of high-income households in private institutions' economies. So long as incomes are growing at the top of the distribution among families who can actually pay all or most of the high tuition costs, revenues can rise along with sticker prices despite increasing discount rates. And at the top of the distribution, incomes certainly have risen: average real household income in the top quintile rose more than $85,000 between 1967 and 2006. Even as incomes at other levels flattened in the final decade of this period, growth in the top quintile continued on at the same pace (DeNavas-Walt and Proctor 2014).[4]

Robust net tuition revenue growth in the decade leading up to the financial crisis testifies to the importance of what economists refer to as "price discrimination." Because they vary along a variety of dimensions, such that families do not view them as perfect substitutes, colleges and universities have a degree of market power, and so they are able to charge families different prices depending on their ability and willingness to pay. Sticker-price growth is offset by financial aid increases for most families, such that net price is largely unaffected. This explains the higher discount rates reported previously. But high-income families do actually pay more as published fees increase. If such families are numerous enough, institutions may experience healthy net tuition revenue growth at the same time that the discount rate rises. From this perspective, rising discount rates are hardly ironclad evidence that something is amiss. Rather, increased discounting can easily point to a college's ever-more-effective price discrimination as high-income families are weaned off of implicit financial aid provided when fees fall short of the average cost of providing an education.

While the high-tuition/high-aid model has been disproportionately practiced by national and elite institutions with high fees, evidence suggests similar principles are increasingly relevant to public institutions as well. The US Department of Education's 2011–12 National Postsecondary Student Aid Study reports family income distributions for students by type of institution attended (Radwin et al. 2013). At four-year doctorate-granting public institutions, 35 percent of students have parents whose incomes top $100,000, while 38 percent report parent incomes less than $60,000. These figures are all but identical to those for private non-doctoral-granting four-year institutions (36 percent and 38 percent, respectively). Even non-doctoral-granting public institutions draw more than one-quarter of their students from families with six-figure incomes.

Since the onset of the Great Recession, states appear to have decided to tap into these pools of family financial resources, shifting the relative burden of educational costs from the state to the students and families benefiting from the education. According to the State Higher Education Executive Officers Association (SHEEO; 2016), inflation-adjusted appropriations per full-time equivalent student fell by an average of 16.6 percent between fiscal years 2008 and 2015. In 45 states, per-student appropriations have fallen, and in 20 of those states the cuts were deeper than 20 percent. Only four states—Alaska, North Dakota, Wyoming, and Illinois—increased per-student appropriations by more than 1 percent, and these outliers only serve to prove the rule. Until recently, soaring oil and gas prices have generated a flood of dollars into state coffers in Alaska, North Dakota, and Wyoming, allowing them to buck all kinds of national budgetary trends. And regarding Illinois, the SHEEO study notes that the 40 percent increase in appropriations actually speaks to the state's underfunding of higher education. Many years of minimal payments to the state's pension program have led to a pension gap of approximately $100 billion. To address this massive pension gap, Illinois earmarked an additional $1.5 billion per year in higher education expenditure to address (partially) the shortfall. After adjusting for what amount to back payments for pensions, funding to operations of Illinois's higher education system have fallen by about 10 percent—right in line with experiences in other states.

In response to dwindling state support, from 2004 through 2014 public four-year colleges and universities increased tuition and fees by 5.7 percent per year, a rate two and a half times that of inflation (DeNavas-Walt and Proctor 2014). As a result, net fee income soared. Between fiscal years 2008 and 2015, the average state saw a 36 percent increase in net fee income from public college and university students (SHEEO 2016). Over the past five years, in 34 states net fee income rose by at least 20 percent. Fee income rose by less than 10 percent in only eight states; at the same time, six posted increases in excess of 50 percent. With state support down and family support on the rise, the share of public educational expenses covered by net fee income rose from just more than one-third in 2009 to 47 percent in 2015. It would seem that public institutions are joining private peers in implementing the high-tuition/high-aid model in which high-income families are of critical importance.

Predicting Numbers of High-Pay College Students

HEDI forecasts can be used to project the number of students with high ability to pay by restricting the sample of young people to those with demographic markers of both willingness and ability to pay. This set of forecasts is a bit speculative because it requires us to identify children as potential high-pay students many years before they even sit their SATs. Instead, the model defines a proxy for full-pay status based on family income and parental education.

Because ability to pay is strongly associated with family income, the HEDI full-pay index begins by identifying American Community Survey children whose families are at the top of the income distribution. Were children of all ages compared to one another, we could easily guess the outcome: older children would be disproportionately represented at the top because their parents are typically older and so are further along in their careers. Proceeding this way would predictably lead to the erroneous prediction that the share of children from high-income families will steadily fall with time. To avoid this bias, the HEDI full-pay index measures family income relative to the distribution found among families with children of the same age. More specifically, a child is coded as "high-income" if her family's income falls in the top 13 percent of families with children her age. For the sake of comparison, in the 2002 Education Longitudinal Study sample of high school sophomores, the 87th-percentile income reached $100,000 (approximately $130,000 in 2016 dollars). While this is not enough to pay the full published fee at most elite schools, it is enough to make a significant contribution toward the cost of education.

In addition to having the ability to pay, full-pay families must have a willingness to make a substantial investment in their child's education. Earlier chapters documented a strong correlation between parental education and a child's propensity to enroll at four-year institutions (and national or elite four-year schools in particular). It would seem that highly educated parents have a greater willingness to fund expensive college experiences for their children. So, to proxy for willingness to pay, the HEDI full-pay index restricts the sample of high-income families to those with strong parental attachment to education as measured by parents' bachelor's degree receipt. In total, a HEDI full-pay student is one whose parents both hold a bachelor's and whose family income lies in the top 13 percent of the distribution found among those in the same birth cohort.

This proxy measure has obvious limitations. Because the income measure is inherently relative, in each birth cohort 13 percent of children will be coded as "high-income." This may make it seem that the measure must follow the education patterns seen in earlier chapters: as more adults take up higher education, more children must be in homes labeled as "potential full-pay families." While such trends are important to the proposed proxy measure, it is more complicated than this critique suggests. Specifically, even if the number of adults with bachelor's degrees increases, the number of couples in which each holds a bachelor's depends on the degree to which marriage partners positively sort based on their education backgrounds. Furthermore, the proposed proxy depends on the correlation between parent education and family income. While a strong association exists in the data, chapter 6 notes that this association has changed dramatically over time. Finally, the total number of children in high-income families with strong parental education will depend on the correlations among fertility, family income, and parental education. These three factors mean that the proposed proxy is not predetermined to follow any particular path.

National Forecasts

The HEDI projects steady growth in the number of young people with the profile of a full-pay student (figure 7.2). The top panel presents forecasts for broad measures of higher education demand—any college and four-year college—along with projections for regional four-year schools. We can anticipate healthy increases in the number of such students over the next decade before a partial reversal at the end of the 2020s due to the birth dearth. Because young people fitting the profile have a high probability of four-year college attendance, projections are similar, whether talking about 18-year-olds, postsecondary enrollees, or four-year attenders. Between 2012 and 2025, the numbers of students fitting the full-pay profile is predicted to rise 30 percent before reversing about 15 percent for a net increase of 10 percent by 2029. Perhaps a bit surprisingly, the model predicts that growth in full-pay recruitment pools will extend to regional four-year institutions as well. In fact, the expected rate of increase through 2025 is anticipated to be slightly larger at regional institutions than at four-year institutions as a whole. Perhaps less surprisingly, the lower panel of the figure plots reasonably strong

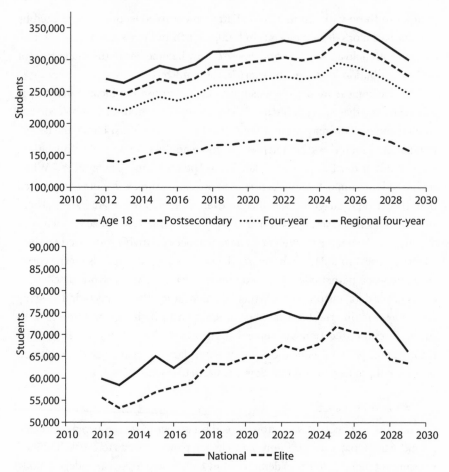

Figure 7.2. Forecasted number of potential full-pay students, by year of high school graduation

growth in full-pay students at national and elite institutions, where such enroll-ments are expected to rise about 25 percent by 2025 before falling back to a net gain of 14 percent.

As seen in earlier chapters, the expansion in students fitting the full-pay pro-file coincides with an overall contraction in the number of total students at most institution types. Together, these forces will increase the full-pay share within the population from around 6.5 percent today to about 7.5 percent in 2029. Among four-year college enrollers, the share of full-pay students is unsurprisingly higher, at around 13 percent, and is expected to increase by three points. While children from high-income/high-education families make up approximately one-third of the current student body at elite institutions, the HEDI does not predict growth among full-pay students to differ from that of elite students in general. As a result, the share of elite students from full-pay backgrounds is not expected to change. By contrast, the share of such students at regional and national four-year schools is expected to rise between three and five percentage points in coming years. So, in the midst of challenging enrollment declines, regional and national institutions will find a bit of relief in their students' abilities to pay.

Local Forecasts

When broken down by census region, regional differences are clear.[5] (Graphs of regional forecasts are available with supplemental materials on the book's website.[6]) Regardless of institution type, the HEDI suggests that students fitting the full-pay profile will increase by approximately 30 percent in the West and South. By contrast, no growth is expected in the Midwest and Northeast. Elite institutions might expect to enjoy slightly more growth in the West and slightly less in the South and Northeast, but in general the patterns of growth in full-pay students are very similar across institution type in all four regions.

In one sense, these geographic decompositions only reinforce one of the messages of chapter 6: institutions dependent on recruitment from the northeastern quadrant of the country will fare less well than those that can draw from elsewhere. But in another sense, the data might be seen as mitigating enrollment concerns raised in that chapter. Regardless of the region, we expect no fewer students from highly educated parents with incomes near the top of the income distribution. Because these students are substantially responsible for higher education's economic model, this data could be taken as a very positive counterpoint to falling enrollment numbers because the financial consequences of falling enrollments will be less pronounced than the drop in student numbers.

Placing these regional forecasts for full-pay students against those for population yields estimates for changes to the share of full-pay students in each region and institution type. For four-year institutions as a group, just as in the population as a whole, the share of young people fitting the full-pay profile is expected to rise by between one and two percentage points in all four regions—from 10 percent to 11 percent in the Northeast and from around 6 percent to around 7 percent in the other three regions. A similar regional pattern is seen among students at regional four-year institutions. In the Northeast, the share of students who are full-pay is expected to rise from 14 percent to 16 percent. The other regions expect similar expansion of the full-pay share, although from a lower base, rising to 12 percent from a current share of 9 percent.

Where geographic variation is most evident is among elite institutions. In this subgroup, the share of students who are full-pay will only rise in the West, rising from 32 percent today to 36 percent in 2029. In the other three regions, the share of full-pay students at elite schools is expected to fall marginally. While this is not to say that the absolute number of full-pay, elite students is falling in the other regions (the model predicts strong growth in the South and effectively no change in the Midwest and Northeast), elite institutions that attract qualified students from the West have a greater chance of drawing a student from a family with the ability to pay all or nearly all of the tuition fees. This finding also amplifies a lesson from chapter 6: most elite institutions may be able to fill their classes without adjusting recruitment strategies, but taking a more flexible approach presents opportunities for a stronger institution. Conversely, many selective schools are committed to enrolling a socioeconomically diverse student body. If that goal is paramount, institutions may prefer to focus their outreach in the Midwest, which is expected to have the fewest full-pay students as a share of all elite-bound students. To the degree that elite schools elect not to "follow the money," second-tier institutions may find even more relief from stresses caused by enrollment pressures as those who trickle down to the second tier disproportionately represent full-pay families.

Implications

If all forecasts rest on assumptions that may fail, this is particularly true when attempting to predict demand from a narrow sliver atop the income distribution. The economy may run into another deep recession or may grow at higher rates than we've seen as of late. Technological change may tilt the labor market to the relative advantage or disadvantage of those with greatest skill. Any of these or more could change the environment in a way that undermines forecasts of full-paying ability and willingness based on present observations.

Even with these necessary caveats, the results in this chapter give evidence for confidence in using the results in chapter 6 to guide institutional decision making. Of particular note, the predicted number of full-pay students is expected to be flat or higher in coming years. That is, the predicted rise in the number of students with characteristics consistent with elite college attendance does not simply represent an increase in bodies with no accompanying means to pay. This is also true (maybe more so) for less selective four-year institutions, which means that the primary challenge facing regional and national schools will be raw demand rather than its composition with respect to fee-paying status. While geographic differences can be observed across census regions, these are modest enough such that the shares of students with full-pay capacity will move more or less in unison across the country. The one exception to this rule may be the exceptional rise of full-pay students in the West for both national and elite institutions. But even this exception largely proves the point: the one geographic anomaly (and that is a stretch, given the magnitudes involved) is found in the market for elite institutions in which students readily travel, and so regional differences are least important.

In this light, the forecasts for full-pay students underscore ideas articulated in chapter 6. Rising numbers of full-pay students may cushion the blow of falling overall demand among regional colleges and universities. Still, the modest changes in full-pay numbers predicted in this chapter are too small to offset the deep declines forecasted for demand as a whole. As in the regional analyses discussed in chapter 6, changes in full-pay demand for regional colleges and universities are expected to be more or less uniform across geography. As a result, we can expect these institutions will often find value in comparing notes with schools working in other regions of the country. Finally, as is the case in the raw numbers of demand, the demand for full-pay students will be somewhat more favorable for institutions of greater selectivity. Given that the full-pay analysis more or less conforms to the broader study of demand, the strategic responses in the next chapter will be discussed largely in the context of total demand.

Chapter Eight

Coping with Change

Strategies for Institutional Response

Given the Higher Education Demand Index data, what is a college president (or admission vice president) to do? As demographic trends transform the higher education landscape over the next 15 years, institutions would do well to take McGee's (2016) perspective: "[T]he changing conditions reshaping the world of higher education in America should lead us neither to gloom nor to despair but rather to the pursuit of opportunity and advantage" (143). Colleges and universities that choose to view enrollment shifts as a challenge whose solution could make them stronger will do much better than those that take a less proactive stance. Clearly, good policy must reflect an individual institution's culture and context, and so it isn't possible to suggest specific strategies that are likely to work for all or even many institutions. Still, drawing on the scholarship of higher education and admissions policy, it is possible to identify a range of general approaches that administrators might consider.

With that goal in mind, possible responses can be grouped roughly under three broad descriptions. The hard-nosed approach accepts as given changing enrollments for the nation as a whole and the institution in particular. Having acknowledged these constraints on student numbers, hard-nosed strategies attempt to grapple directly with resulting budgetary pressures by increasing revenue and/or cutting costs. By contrast, the hopeful approach contemplates futures that reach beyond HEDI predictions by looking for policies that increase attendance rates above those assumed in the model. This path refuses to take the model forecasts as given for either the nation or the institution. Between these two poles lies a nimble path that presumes that the HEDI forecasts are true for the nation as a whole but seeks ways for an individual institution to beat the odds by carefully adjusting recruitment efforts to auspicious new student pools. Institutional context will dictate which of these paths is best suited for an individual school, and many may find it necessary to create hybrid paths by taking parts of more than one broad approach.

Budget Management: The Hard-Nosed Approach

The first strategies to be considered are likely to be the most familiar. As noted in chapter 7, reductions in state funding have nudged public institutions (and some competing private schools as well) in the direction of the high-tuition/ high-aid pricing long practiced at national and elite colleges and universities. As McGuinness (2016) rightly observes, future increases in Medicaid costs promise only greater pressure on state legislators to balance their budgets through reductions in higher education outlays. Johnstone (2016) goes even further, suggesting that some state higher education systems may welcome reductions in state aid because it might free them from the political and social constraints inherent in being "state supported institutions" (326). Vermont may effectively be there already, with family net tuition payments accounting for 85 percent of educational revenues (SHEEO 2016). If present financial pressures nudge administrators to consider the high-tuition/high-aid model, the 25 percent reduction in demand for regional four-year schools in the East North Central and New England may shove them in that direction.

Of course, radical changes to pricing strategy are hardly costless or risk free. First, it isn't clear that net revenue would increase. While high-income families have the ability to pay much more than current tuition rates at many regional colleges and universities, so long as low-cost alternatives remain, those families will have a strong incentive to look elsewhere if their first choice increases its comprehensive fee. Ironically, if relatively few schools take an active approach to falling demand by adopting a high-tuition/high-aid model, then it may be that the passive schools that stick their head in the sand and do nothing actually fair better (though perhaps not well), as they benefit from a steady stream of students seeking to avoid new, higher tuition rates elsewhere. Johnstone (2016) worries about the societal consequences of such rematching of students and schools. First, if public schools adopt the pricing strategy of national and elite schools, Johnstone predicts that the "most attractive and able" students from high-income families will no longer have an incentive to consider public institutions. As a result, the trend over recent decades toward greater sorting on student ability that is documented by Hoxby (2009) may be exacerbated, resulting in lower-quality public institutions. In addition, Johnstone worries that students from low-income families (many of whose parents have little experience with higher education) might be so overwhelmed by high sticker prices as to be discouraged from looking closely enough to see available financial aid. The result could be a reversal of recently rising attendance rates among underrepresented income and racial/ethnic groups. Most fundamentally, Johnstone contends that the public adoption of the high-tuition/high-aid pricing model undermines the argument that education has public good elements.

If enrollment reductions create budget shortfalls that cannot be addressed by increasing revenue, then those adopting the hard-nosed approach must turn to expenditure reductions to fill any remaining gaps. Because staffing costs account for 60 to 70 percent of college and university budgets, and instructional compensation comprises half of this subtotal (Desrochres and Kirshstein 2014), meaningful cuts will almost surely include reductions in the number of teachers. The 18-to-1 student-to-faculty ratio estimated at the end of chapter 4 can be used to size up the implications of falling enrollments for the demand for faculty of different institution types in different areas of the county. At two-year institutions, forecasted enrollment reductions suggest losses of more than 8,000 faculty positions. Half of those will be lost in the Pacific and East North Central, where more than 2,000 lines might be cut in each division. Another 1,000 to 1,500 full-time equivalents (FTE) might be eliminated in the Middle Atlantic and East South Central.

If proportional to student numbers, the loss of faculty at regional four-year institutions will be equally large, if not more so—a loss of more than 9,000 positions nationally. In contrast to the case of two-year colleges, reductions in regional four-year faculty FTE would be more concentrated, with approximately 60 percent falling (more or less equally) in the East North Central and Middle Atlantic. Even accounting for the fraction of these lost positions that might be offset by additional hiring at national and elite institutions, a proportionate reduction in faculty would make for a very challenging faculty job market for years to come.

While staff reductions can take many forms, the high price associated with tenure lines leaves relatively little space between discussions of instructional staff savings and threats to tenure. As with changes to the pricing model, this pressure to reduce faculty costs is nothing new. The American Association of University Professors reports a steady decline in the share of instructional staff who are full-time tenured and tenure-track faculty from 44 percent of total instructional staff in 1975 to less than 25 percent in 2011 (Curtis and Thornton 2013). What is new in some locations and for some institution types will be the magnitude of coming enrollment pressures, which will be more intense than any recent experience.

Altbach (2016a) is right that tenure's demise has been predicted before (most recently in the 1970s and 1990s), but the widespread discussion of tenure's costs and benefits suggests that long-standing models of instruction are up for debate (Blumenstyk 2015, Bok 2013, Johnstone 2016, and O'Neil 2016). HEDI projections presented in chapters 4 through 6 may supply evidence for administrators' argument that adjunct instructors provide institutions with needed flexibility. The argument for avoiding the long-term commitments of tenure will be made even stronger by the fact that in many markets we expect a brief rise in demand during the early 2020s, before a precipitous drop caused by the birth dearth. However, the consequences of increasing the share of adjunct positions extend far beyond budgets. Institutions that balance budgets by supplanting tenure face risks associated with diluted faculty governance (Blumenstyk 2015), diminished academic freedom (O'Neil 2016), and low morale stemming from financial insecurity for the professoriate (Blumenstyk 2015). Most importantly, research suggests that the use of part-time teaching staff can erode educational quality through grade inflation and lower retention (Bok 2013).

While it may be impossible for some institutions to avoid entirely the pains of faculty reductions, depending on the implementation some potential benefits can partially offset the costs. With thousands fewer students to teach, a reversal of recent expansion in adjunct lines would increase the share of tenured/tenure-track faculty without reducing student-faculty ratios. Moreover, even if states continue to reduce financial support for higher education, if enrollments fall at a faster pace than funding does, public institutions may simultaneously scratch back some recent losses in per-pupil spending. In writing this, I do not mean to diminish the pain associated with such a transition—particularly for staff who lose jobs. There is simply no way to avoid significant disruption as the number of students east of the Mississippi who enroll at regional four-year schools falls by approximately 20 percent in less than a decade's time. Still, many scholars would argue that it would be a good thing if, despite that pain, an institution came out the other side of the birth dearth with a stronger tenure system and slightly higher per-pupil expenditures from the state.

Technology may provide another avenue to reduce staff costs through increased teaching productivity. Perna and Ruiz (2016) argue that while computer technology has radically altered some aspects of higher education, it "has had relatively little impact on instructional approaches at most colleges and universities" (440). They, along with Johnstone (2016) and Bok (2013), note the potential for online technology to overcome higher education's "cost disease" by empowering faculty to teach effectively to larger numbers of students.[1] While massive open online courses (MOOCs) have generated the most media attention in this area, a wide range of blended learning tools attempts to improve teaching efficiency. For example, by posting lecture material online and reserving face-to-face contact for more active forms of learning, a single professor might teach two sections of students with less than twice the time and effort. Without doubt, online technologies can and have provided better education at lower costs in some areas. For example, Perna and Ruiz (2016) cite webinars with alumni experts and advising tools that make it easy for students to see remaining graduation requirements, contemplate alternative majors, and design curricular plans.

As real as these gains have been, many questions surround the more radical claim that online systems will allow for effective learning despite very high student-to-faculty ratios. Relatively few studies have carefully examined student learning outcomes in online as compared to more common face-to-face environments. (See Bernard et al. 2014 and Means et al. 2010 for reviews of the literature.) What work has been done has defined learning in very narrow, content-based terms that fail to capture many important parts of any meaningful definition of a college education. Bok (2013) carefully enumerates other losses students may experience if we decide to abandon traditional teaching methods: online media provide fewer opportunities for students to be exposed to and to understand alternative viewpoints expressed by peers in classroom discussions, create less sense of community (which is a critical factor in student retention studies), and impede informal conversations with faculty and peers that often lead to new insights or even new academic and career goals. Moreover, if the budgetary pains of enrollment reduction are addressed by increasing student-to-faculty ratios, then faculty cuts will need to be even more extreme than those described previously, amplifying the institutional costs of that transition.

In the long run, technology may solve higher education's cost disease, but it seems unlikely that the long run will arrive in time to provide meaningful help to administrators grappling with the massive demographic changes coming in the next 10 to 15 years. The use of computers and VHS tapes to provide individualized instruction with fewer faculty inputs dates back at least to the 1980s. Were such technologies capable of supporting high-quality student learning, surely we would see substantial market penetration by now. While the number of participants in large online courses is impressive enough to grab headlines, fewer than 10 percent of colleges and universities currently offer even one MOOC, and a decreasing share of administrators view them as sustainable (Perna and Ruiz 2016). Moreover, those institutions that have invested heavily in attempts to make MOOCs work achieve significantly lower retention rates. Realistically, at best the selective application of online learning technology will be a measured part of a sound response to coming enrollment declines.

Increasing College Attendance Rates: The Hopeful Path

Administrators uncomfortable with significant changes to revenue and/or cost models must instead look for ways to offset expected declines in the number of young people by increasing attendance rates. This can be accomplished in two ways: by reaching beyond traditional students or by increasing attendance rates within the traditional student population. When considering the former, McGee (2016) argues we can learn from institutions' responses to falling numbers of high school graduates in the 1970s. While rising returns to education helped attract a larger share of students to higher education, colleges and universities also helped their own cause by reaching out to new student groups. To some degree, schools simply extended established trends. For instance, women's share in postsecondary enrollment drifted upward, from 35 percent in the mid-1950s to just more than 40 percent by the end of the 1960s. With fewer high school graduates, colleges were more than happy to accelerate this trend, increasing women's share to more than 50 percent by 1979 (NCES 2015, table 303.10). At the same time, higher education sought to create more or less new markets. Postsecondary enrollments of students older than 35 doubled between 1970 and 1980, and added another 50 percent to their number by 1990 (NCES 2015, table 303.40).

Having pulled these levers to address the last birth dearth, institutions will need to look elsewhere for opportunities to increase matriculation rates in the future. Today, when women account for 60 percent of enrollments and those older than 30 account for 25 percent, we must wonder how much more demand (if any) can be generated from these sources. Bok (2013) and Kolodny (1998) suggest retirees may enroll for the simple pleasure of learning new things or gaining a deeper understanding of passions identified later in life. While an intriguing idea, Kolodny wisely notes that catering to a market with such different motivations, experiences, and needs requires that we answer questions that higher education has yet to even pose. For nonresidential institutions, a less dramatic step might be to use blended learning to teach students of all ages whose family or employment commitments make it difficult to show up regularly to class at a particular time and place (Bok 2013).

International students represent another growing market (Altbach 2016b, Blumenstyk 2015, Kumar and Hurwitz 2015, and McGee 2016), and technology may make it easier to reach them than in the past (Bok 2013). The number of foreign students studying in the United States has increased by 37 percent since 2010, pushing the international enrollment share to almost 5 percent (Institute of International Education 2015). Most of this growth took place at flagship universities and private, nonprofit four-year institutions, though the level of international representation at these schools is not much higher than that at other public four-year colleges and universities. Interestingly, expansion to international students also constituted a part of higher education's response to the drop in high school graduations in the 1970s. During that decade, the share of international students, which had been steady during the two previous decades, abruptly rose by 50 percent (from less than 1.7 percent of all higher education enrollments to almost 2.6 percent). Fifty years later, we may see a similar expansion in the 2020s.

Surely, outreach to nontraditional and international students will play some part in higher education's response to American demographic change, and for some institutions such changes may entirely offset softening domestic demand. However, given the depth of the coming decline, those who hope that higher education can recruit its way out of enrollment contractions must also contemplate ways to increase college attendance within the traditional, domestic student population—either through recruitment efforts, public policy (see chapter 10 for more on this possibility), or both. Already, admissions officers are reaching out to new domestic markets by translating admissions materials into other languages, creating virtual campus tours, and using alumni interviews to reach subgroups that might not make a campus visit (Hoover 2013a).

By altering probability estimates incorporated in the HEDI model, the framework can be used to explore the potential and limits of increased college enrollment rates as a response to coming demographic change. The analysis that follows focuses on two thought experiments designed to capture expansion in attendance rates:

- What if recruitment and government policy changes targeted students from lower-income families such that effects of income on enrollment were largely reduced? Specifically, I alter the probit regression parameters on income in both high school persistence and college attendance, eliminating half of the estimated coefficient difference between the highest family income group—that is, the one with the strongest higher education attachment—and each of the other seven income groups.

• What if recruitment and government policy changes sought to close attendance gaps across race? In this hypothetical world, all race/ ethnicity model coefficients are moved one-half of the way from their estimated values to those of Asian Americans—the group with greatest higher education attachment.

For two-year institutions, comparing the status quo forecast from chapter 5 with those of the two alternatives yields decidedly different results. Figure 8.1 presents two-year enrollment maps under the status quo and both thought experiments. In the figure, it is evident that government and higher education policies that mitigate differences by race/ethnicity would marginally improve forecasts, while those intended to mitigate differences across income would make two-year

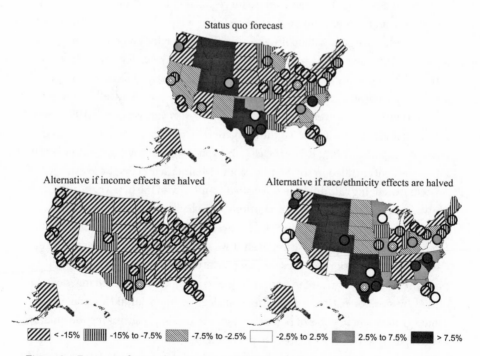

Figure 8.1. Forecasted growth in two-year college attendance under status quo and alternative policies that mitigate effects of income and race/ethnicity, 2012 to 2029

enrollment figures substantially worse. The reason for this is simple. While Asian American students disproportionately attend four-year institutions, they remain high users of two-year schools as well. As a result, were other race/ethnicity groups more like Asians, the net result would be larger two-year enrollments. By contrast, high-income families tilt toward four-year attendance at the expense of two-year matriculation. So, policies that reduce the effects of economic background would result in smaller two-year enrollments—so much so that nearly every location would see deep contraction by 2029.

Looking more closely at the potential for increasing attendance by better outreach to Hispanics and non-Hispanic blacks, it is clear that this strategy is more auspicious in some regions than others. Two-year colleges in the South Atlantic will be able to entirely reverse losses if they can draw in these underrepresented groups. In the Northeast, equalization of attendance by race/ethnicity will not entirely offset losses, but in the West North Central and Middle Atlantic it will be close. These findings provide a potential way forward for two-year schools in these areas of the country.

Figure 8.2 repeats the same exercise for regional four-year colleges, with decidedly different outcomes. Unlike the forecasts for two-year schools, closing income and race/ethnicity gaps will do little to alter the geographic contours of education demand in the next 15 years. To be sure, efforts to make college attendance patterns more uniformly like high-income and Asian American families will generally increase enrollments. (The exceptions to this rule are nearly all found in the Pacific division, and even there the downward revision is modest.) However, forecasts under both alternative futures generally mimic those in the status quo baseline: the Midwest and Northeast can expect significant contraction, while growth is concentrated in the Southeast and Mountain and Pacific West.

Acknowledging this difference, a critical similarity in the hypothetical futures of two- and regional four-year institutions is probably much more important. In wide swaths of the country (and the Midwest and Northeast in particular), the forecasts remain deeply negative, even if we were to dramatically reduce attendance gaps. Institutions of these types recruiting in affected regions would be poorly served by unwarranted optimism that coming enrollment changes can be erased by state or national programs that deepen financial aid to underrepresented groups. These pools of potential students are simply shrinking too quickly to be replenished by even aggressive policy change.

It could be argued that the hypothetical worlds forecasted for regional four-year institutions are overly pessimistic. The thought experiments consider a

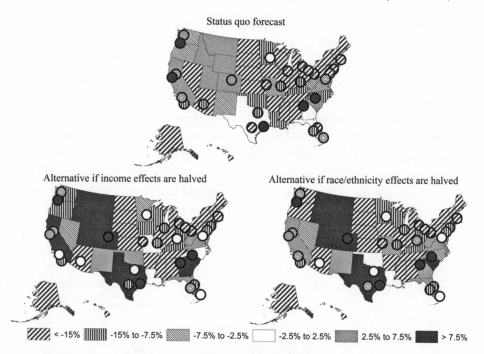

Figure 8.2. Forecasted growth in regional four-year college attendance under status quo and alternative policies that mitigate effects of income and race/ethnicity, 2012 to 2029

society-wide shift toward the attendance patterns found among high-income and Asian American families. Because these groups disproportionately attend national and elite schools, the model therefore forecasts rapid attendance growth at these top-ranked institutions: enrollments at these schools would increase by approximately one-third in both hypothetical worlds. As a result, if we were to halve income effects, forecasted aggregate enrollments at four-year institutions as a whole increase in 51 of the 63 locations. The effect of halving race/ethnicity effects would be only slightly less widespread with increases in 42 locations. Because it seems quite unlikely that national and elite schools would expand by 30 percent in such a short time, regional four-year colleges would benefit from the resulting surplus. This would improve the outlook from that presented in figure 8.2. While this is true, locations expected to lose four-year students in aggregate are concentrated such that, even with large reductions in income or race/ethnicity gaps, the hypothetical forecasts for broad four-year enrollment are flat or lower in the East North Central, Middle Atlantic, and New England census divisions. Again, in the areas of the country with the greatest number of regional four-year schools, it is hard to imagine that even aggressive recruitment or public policy changes can overcome the demographic arithmetic.

From what has just been noted, we should not make too much of the thought experiment forecasts for national and elite institutions. After all, it seems highly unlikely that the attendance gradient across income will be halved among elite schools in just 15 years. Even if it were, schools would surely not increase class sizes by 30 percent or more. Still, the forecasts mapped in figure 8.3 point to several important lessons. First, halving either the race/ethnicity or income gradient would reverse negative trends in the Midwest and Northeast. In these regions, where status quo estimates point to deep reductions in the number of students headed to top-100 schools, halving income or race/ethnicity effects would more than eliminate the loss. Even if we believe that policy changes can't realistically achieve such remarkable effects, the point is clear. Through greater recruitment of underrepresented groups or innovations in government policy,

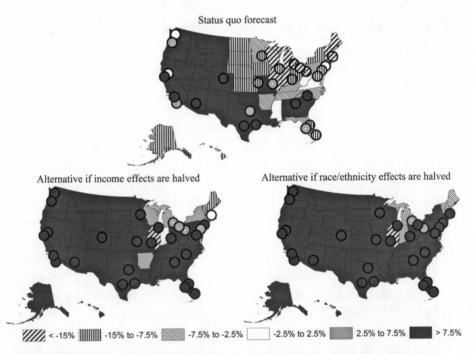

Figure 8.3. Forecasted growth in combined national and elite four-year college attendance under status quo and alternative policies that mitigate effects of income and race/ethnicity, 2012 to 2029

national and elite institutions drawing from the Midwest and Northeast could substantially reduce the disturbance of coming demographic change. Thus these schools can reasonably choose between reaching out to new geographic markets or focusing more sharply on underrepresented groups in markets where they have historically enjoyed success.

A second takeaway focuses on the few locations that continue to anticipate reductions in national and elite student numbers despite the imagined progress in reaching underrepresented groups. Specifically, HEDI forecasts remain negative in Detroit, Michigan, Illinois, Vermont, New Hampshire, and Maine, and are weak in Pittsburgh and Indiana. National and elite schools currently drawing primarily from these markets need to accept a hard truth: even energetic outreach to underrepresented groups supported by aggressive government policy is unlikely to offset the effects of coming demographic change. These markets are simply too weak, and institutions heavily dependent on them will need to work quickly to diversify geographically their recruitment pools or find themselves at a distinct competitive disadvantage to peers.

Whether expanding into new markets or recruiting greater numbers of lower-income and underrepresented minorities, institutions that pursue the hopeful path of increased attendance rates need to prepare for concomitant changes in student support, pedagogy, and curriculum that may be required when working with new student groups. Smith (2016) notes that these changes are already well under way, though "a great deal of work continues on access, student success and support, campus climate, curricular and pedagogical transformation, and the diversification of faculty and staff" (378–79). (Neumann and Campbell [2016] similarly argue that we must expect to change how we teach when we change who we teach.) Online instructional tools such as blended learning technology may prove to be of some help by creating greater scheduling flexibility for students with jobs or small children. In addition, online content could be designed to support college students with academic gaps. Whatever the means, institutions that respond to enrollment challenges by expanding their recruitment pool will want to plan for new forms of student support.

Strategic Redeployment of Recruitment Resources: The Nimble Path

Each in their own way, hard-nosed solutions predicated on aggressive budget management and hopeful solutions requiring outreach to new student communities are likely to be fundamentally disruptive. Some schools may be able to avoid making these choices through careful reallocation of recruitment activity designed to offset expected enrollment reductions in current prospective student pools with new or deeper penetration into others. While this is an appealing idea, each institution must honestly assesses whether this approach is truly viable, acknowledging from the outset that only a minority of institutions will succeed by rethinking recruitment strategies. First, this approach presumes that institutions can identify potential new and growing markets. Citing data on students' willingness to travel to college like that presented in previous chapters, McGee (2016) suggests that most four-year schools should not expect much recruitment success more than 500 miles from campus. Most two-year colleges presumably face a much smaller recruitment sphere. Because enrollment forecasts show strong spatial correlation, many institutions facing declining recruitment pools can point to no realistic alternative, nearby market where growth can be expected. Even institutions identifying potential new and growing recruitment pools must recognize that in a time of declining aggregate enrollments, recruitment is a zero-sum game; the few pockets of growth will be recruited by many schools, and yet each student will enroll at only one.

The most obvious candidates for recruitment redeployment will be found among the national colleges and universities. With likely excess growth in demand for elite schools, it seems quite possible that some second-tier schools will benefit from trickle-down enrollments. But these are not the only schools who may find ways to expand their reach into new pools. For example, community colleges in the Pacific West facing moderate to strong contractions may attempt to tap into growth in regional four-year students by offering a version of the community college baccalaureate degree described by Bahr and Gross (2016). Similarly, regional four-year institutions in the West South Central may attempt to reach students who might otherwise be bound for two-year schools. Finally, some regional institutions may attempt to break through McGee's 500-mile boundary— targeting growing student numbers in the West, perhaps—through the use of distance education and online instruction. For institutions seeing these or other opportunities, HEDI forecasts in prior chapters can inform successful attempts to meet enrollment challenges through strategic recruitment practices.

For institutions placing a bet on recruitment redeployment, this process surely begins with a frank assessment of the expected enrollment risk. While admissions officers may have local information that makes them think they will do better or worse than the average school, a weighted average of HEDI forecasts provides an approximation of what to expect in the next 15 years. For example, consider a national four-year college drawing students exclusively from the following areas: Indiana, Illinois, Chicago, Iowa, Missouri, and St. Louis. Suppose that Chicago and St. Louis each account for 30 percent of enrollments, while each nonmetropolitan area accounts for 10 percent. If the school's enrollments from each of these areas changed in proportion to the forecasted demand for national institutions, this school would stand to see enrollments decrease by 19 percent. Of course, this is not a forecast of the realized change in the size of the student body. First, confronted with a shrinking pool of applicants, this school would likely increase acceptance rates (with the attendant reduction in student quality). Conversely, competition from other institutions facing similar challenges may cause our hypothetical school's pool to shrink even faster; in the context of a nationwide contraction, admissions departments can't simply expect "their share" of students in any market. Still, the HEDI-generated forecast can distinguish the fates of a school like this one from another that draws equally from the five California markets where enrollments might be expected to grow by 12.6 percent.

Having sized up the challenge, institutions can look for potential new recruitment pools. The first location they may want to consider are those at the intersection of "markets we already draw from" and "markets that are expected to grow." In the case of our hypothetical school in the Midwest, if it could alter its recruitment profile so that the shares of students drawn from Illinois, Indiana, and Chicago fell by five percentage points each and were replaced by five-point increases in the three other markets, then their enrollments would only fall by 16 percent. For this school, the nonurban Missouri market bears additional attention. Because demand for elite colleges in rural Missouri is expected to more than double—an increase of more than 500 students—it is likely that some of these students will trickle down to national schools. With an existing presence in the area, our hypothetical school might reasonably hope to have an advantage in recruiting from this growing pool.

Given the size of the expected enrollment gap for our hypothetical school, simply reallocating recruitment energies in already established markets is not likely to be enough. Which new markets are most auspicious will depend in part on institution-specific experiences and culture: In areas with a growing population, where can we find young people whose interests and goals match our institutional identity? If this were not all hard enough, it will be made substantially more complicated by the actions of other institutions. With competitors simultaneously scrambling to find new student pools, a successful strategy will also need to anticipate competitors' actions. When going head-to-head in recruitment, against which schools do we typically win and against which schools do we typically lose? Highly effective admissions departments will expand into markets where future competition is against the former and will avoid costly expansions that put themselves in greater competition with the latter.

While strategic recruitment may initially seem preferable to hard-nosed budget management or attempts to increase college attendance rates, it should be clear at this point that most schools will not be able to resolve recruitment shortfalls by finding college-bound students in new and growing markets. The overall contraction is simply too large and the competition too great for many to succeed. Moreover, the negative consequences of failure may be great at schools that make no other changes in preparation for coming demand shifts. Those that beat these odds are likely to be characterized by exceptional agility. They will experiment with recruitment in new territories, cherry-pick students who trickle down due to excess demand for other institution types, nimbly pivot away from fierce competitors toward better peer matchups, and generally accept the necessity for repeated adaptation.

Institutions as Vehicles for Societal Change

In Adam Smith's (1776) seminal work on economics, *The Wealth of Nations*, he memorably argues that, despite nonaltruistic motives, individuals' self-interested pursuits serve to maximize social welfare. It is as if an "invisible hand" guides them to an end that is much greater than any individual's aim. Many of the options explored in this chapter have a similar feel. Though driven by local concerns of financial solvency or recruitment classes with stronger academic profiles, the initiatives discussed above also generate broader impacts by enhancing efficiency, extending the benefits of a college education to underrepresented groups, and improving the match between applicants and institutions. All of these are outcomes of great interest to national and state policymakers who are responsible for reaching societal goals. Just as colleges' and universities' actions can influence state and national policy outcomes, by targeting goals of greater productivity and equality, the actions of policymakers can be very important to the success of higher education institutions. Up to this point, the discussion has only indirectly considered these broader, societal goals and policymaking. The next chapters look at these questions more carefully, using the HEDI to explore how innovations in public policy might affect college-going in general and among underrepresented groups in particular.

Chapter Nine

Anticipated Higher Education Attendance

The Policymaker's Perspective

After five chapters focusing on the perspective of higher education institutions, this chapter shifts to consider the implications for the nation and its workforce preparation. It is important to note that this new topic requires that we turn much of the analysis inside out. Specifically, the previous chapters explore forecasts of the number and composition of students who will matriculate to college campuses and the demographic makeup of the college-going population. Much of the analysis answered questions of the form: What fraction of attenders are from such-and-such group? While policymakers are not uninterested in the challenges faced by institutions of higher education, they are at least as interested in the experience of citizens as a whole. Rather than looking at what groups lie within the college-going population, policymakers want to know how much of the population is college educated. Similarly, they ask whether we are preparing a workforce equipped to compete in the twenty-first century. In addition, those interested in social equality may focus on gaps in college attendance rates between racial/ethnic or income groups.

Questions of workforce preparation and college attendance by underrepresented groups are deeply intertwined. Given the rising share of nonmajority populations, it may be all but impossible to ensure that the country trains a sufficient number of skilled workers without substantially mitigating enrollment gaps that exist today. While the United States used to sit atop the world in the rate of four-year college completion, by the 2000s other countries leapt ahead so that today's US graduation rate sits at the average of all OECD countries. With less than 40 percent of young people completing a four-year program, the United States lags far behind many European peers, where half or more earn degrees (OECD 2015). Analysts estimate we would need to increase degree production by approximately 40 percent to meet workforce needs in coming years (Auguste et al. 2010, Carnevale et al. 2010). While US college attendance rates have risen more than 50 percent since the 1970s, that metric has plateaued at about 65 percent for the last decade or so (NCES 2016, tables 219.75 and 302.30). So, whether motivated by concerns for rising inequality or worries that we are not graduating enough educated workers to meet the economy's demands, many see a national interest in reducing educational attainment gaps. The analysis in this chapter focuses on three specific underrepresented groups: racial/ethnic minorities, students from low-income families, and those whose parents have little or no college experience.

Past trends in educational attainment in these groups offer a useful context for the forecasts presented later in this chapter. From 1972 through the mid-1990s, the percentage of non-Hispanic whites in their late 20s who had attended some college steadily rose from just more than 40 percent to approximately 65 percent, where it has since remained steady.[1] For the first 15 years of this period, attendance rates among non-Hispanic blacks and Hispanics remained flat at about 30 percent, resulting in a widening racial gap as compared to non-Hispanic whites—from about 10 percentage points in 1972 to almost 20 points by 1985. However, beginning in the mid-1980s increases in attendance rates among non-Hispanic blacks kept pace with non-Hispanic whites, and by 2000 the postsecondary enrollment rate among blacks exceeded that of Hispanics by more than 15 points. Since the turn of the century, however, Hispanic matriculations have soared, growing at a faster rate than that for non-Hispanics, such that in 2011 Hispanics had closed the gap with non-Hispanic blacks. In fact, both underrepresented groups made up ground with respect to non-Hispanic whites, and today the attendance gap stands at only five percentage points, the lowest it has been in the past four decades.[2]

Similar, widespread educational gains have been made across income classes. The share of children from low-income families who attend at least some college has steadily increased, from less than 25 percent in the mid-1970s to 45 percent in recent years.[3] While racial attendance gaps appear to be closing, by contrast the income gap has been very consistent, with college attendance rates among children of high-income families exceeding those of low-income and middle-income peers by 35 and 20 percentage points, respectively. Nevertheless, in absolute terms access for low-income students has clearly risen. (This conclusion is also reached by other more formal studies. These figures are roughly comparable with those reported by other authors. For example, see Carneiro and Heckman 2002, Ellwood and Kane 2000, Haveman and Smeeding 2006.)

In the context of these impressive gains in college attendance among underrepresented racial/ethnic minorities and income groups, changes in attendance rates within parental education groups appear quite modest at best. Among those today ages 25 to 29 whose parents do not hold a bachelor's degree, only slightly more than 50 percent have attended college—little better than the 43 percent attendance rate reported in the mid-1970s.[4] Over the same period, attendance rates among those with two parental bachelor's degrees remained steady, at 94 percent. And attendance among those with one parental bachelor's degree actually fell from around 85 percent to approximately 75 percent.

Some considering these observations may find it puzzling that attendance rates are rising in every race/ethnicity and income group and yet are more or less steady across parental education categories. In fact, the apparent lack of progress across parent education groups is misleading. The seeming stasis is largely driven by changes in the composition of the population. As more and more parents acquire four-year postsecondary degrees in response to economic demand (see evidence in chapters 2 and 6), some children, who in the past would have been found among families with low parent education, today live with one or two parents with a bachelor's degree. Similarly, some children who in the past would have reported one parent with a bachelor's degree now report two. Given this compositional change, it is entirely possible for the probability of college attendance to increase for every individual while the share of college-going children falls in every subgroup defined by parent education.[5] In the context of the dramatic shift toward higher parental education, the attendance patterns within groups is actually quite encouraging. Apparently, improvements in access were strong enough to overcome strong compositional effects.

In summation, over recent decades we have seen substantial increases in attachment to higher education within all race/ethnicity and income groups. While the income gaps have been relatively steady, differences by race/ethnicity have closed markedly in the past 20 years. Even the modest gains within parental education groups point to expanding college access. Recurring calls for new policies to increase educational access speak more to the importance of a college education than to reversals or failures in recent decades.

Higher Education Demand Index Forecast Principles

Before looking at HEDI forecasts of educational attainment for the population as a whole and within underrepresented groups, it will be helpful to discuss the implications of HEDI methods for the interpretation of the results. The foundation of the HEDI model is backward looking. That is, the index combines observations of college-going from the recent past with demographic data to predict college-going patterns in the future. As chapter 3 notes, to the degree that relationships between demographic variables and college-going probabilities change in the future, HEDI forecasts will systematically differ from actual higher education choices. While this is inherently true of all forecast models, some readers may wonder whether this means that forecasts of college-going within underrepresented groups are predetermined to show no expected change. If we assume, for example, that the differences in college-going probability associated with race/ethnicity are the same tomorrow as they are today, then how can the share of college-attending Hispanics differ from that seen today? While understandable, this line of reasoning loses sight of the multidimensional nature of the forecasting model. Even though the direct effect of, say, race/ethnicity is assumed to be constant, the correlations between race/ethnicity and other predictors may change. For instance, if parental education is deeper among Hispanic families with infants than that of Hispanic families with teenagers, we would expect the HEDI model to forecast rising educational attainment among Hispanic children as the effects of parental education roll out over time. In this way, changes to the distributions of sex (an unlikely source of variation over time), geography, parental education, family composition, and position in the cohort's income distribution within an underrepresented group can alter forecasts of educational attainment in these subgroups.

Finally, as noted in chapter 3, forecast reliability is inherently reduced when the data are parsed into finer and finer categories. The number of American Community Survey individuals in any given geographic region of any given race/ethnicity acquiring any given level of education can be quite small. To reduce forecast noise resulting from small sample sizes, when examining attendance within population subgroups the following projections are limited to the four census regions and group students into two three-year birth cohorts: students in the high school classes of 2012–2014 and 2027–2029.

National and Regional Forecasts for College Attendance Rates

Overall, HEDI predicts that the recent plateau in college attendance rates will continue into the foreseeable future. Essentially, the shifts toward low-attendance populations in the Hispanic southwest are offset by an increase in the number of families with high levels of parental education. In 15 years, 63 percent of all young people are expected to enroll in some college—compared to 64 percent in 2012. Similarly flat trends are anticipated in all nine census divisions. So, while the dominant narrative may induce excess hand-wringing about possibly cratering attendance rates by overemphasizing only a part of the demographic story—the shifts in geography and race/ethnicity—unless something changes we should not expect to meet goals for a more highly trained workforce.

When HEDI forecasts are broken down by institution type, however, they do produce some interesting variation, at least at the level of the census division. At the national level, both two- and four-year attendance rates appear steady: the model forecasts no change between today and 2029 in either figure, with 28 percent and 41 percent of students attending two- and four-year institutions, respectively. However, at the divisional level the model anticipates regression toward the national mean. Change is most pronounced in the Pacific West and New England, the divisions with the lowest and highest four-year attendance rates, respectively. In the former, four-year attendance rates are expected to increase by five points, from 33 percent to 38 percent. At the same time, high-attendance New England expects slightly lower four-year enrollment rates. In total, the gap between these divisions is expected to fall from 20 points today to only 13 points in 2029. The model also anticipates a mirror-image reversion to the national mean in divisional two-year college attendance rates. So, nationwide we expect to see little change in national attendance rates regardless of institution type, but regions will become much more alike over the next 15 years.

College Attendance within Race/Ethnicity Subgroups

As noted in chapter 2, current college attendance rates differ markedly by race/ethnicity. The upper panel of table 9.1, which differentiates current attendance rates by institution type, provides a little more detail on the differences across groups. More than three-quarters of Asian Americans attend college of some type; this rate is about one-third higher than that among Hispanics and non-Hispanic blacks. These gaps are not driven by two-year college attendance,

Table 9.1 Forecasted college attendance rates among racial/ethnic subpopulations by institution type and census region, 2013 and 2028

Type	Race/ethnicity	Nation (%)	West (%)	Midwest (%)	Northeast (%)	South (%)
				2013		
Any	Non-Hispanic white	69	71	70	73	65
	Non-Hispanic black	55	60	55	60	52
	Hispanic	57	57	58	61	55
	Asian American	77	77	77	76	77
2-year	Non-Hispanic white	29	34	31	24	29
	Non-Hispanic black	26	34	27	21	25
	Hispanic	30	35	28	23	26
	Asian American	28	34	25	20	25
Regional 4-year	Non-Hispanic white	37	34	37	41	35
	Non-Hispanic black	31	29	30	38	30
	Hispanic	26	21	29	34	29
	Asian American	41	34	45	50	45
National/elite	Non-Hispanic white	13	10	13	17	12
	Non-Hispanic black	4	3	4	5	3
	Hispanic	5	4	7	8	6
	Asian American	23	19	29	27	25
				2028		
Any	Non-Hispanic white	69	71	69	72	67
	Non-Hispanic black	52	57	51	58	50
	Hispanic	56	57	54	61	54
	Asian American	82	82	82	82	81
2-year	Non-Hispanic white	28	32	29	23	28
	Non-Hispanic black	24	29	25	22	24
	Hispanic	29	34	27	23	26
	Asian American	28	33	25	21	25
Regional 4-year	Non-Hispanic white	37	36	36	42	36
	Non-Hispanic black	30	30	27	36	29
	Hispanic	26	22	25	35	27
	Asian American	45	38	48	53	47
National/ elite	Non-Hispanic white	14	11	14	18	13
	Non-Hispanic black	4	5	4	5	4
	Hispanic	6	4	6	8	6
	Asian American	33	28	37	37	35

which is (more or less) equally prevalent across race/ethnicity groups: in all groups, about one-third of students matriculate to a two-year college within two years of high school completion. Variation is more evident at four-year colleges in general and national and elite colleges in particular. Almost one-quarter of Asian Americans attend national or elite schools, an attendance rate almost twice that of non-Hispanic whites and four or five times that of Hispanics and non-Hispanic blacks.

With the exception of college attendance among Asian Americans (discussed in detail in what follows), the HEDI forecasts only small changes in college attendance rates within racial/ethnic subgroups over the next 15 years. The lower panel of table 9.1 presents these projections broken down by institution type. Attendance rates in the Hispanic community are expected to be flat in nearly all regions for nearly all college types. The one possible exception to this rule may be found in the Midwest, where college attendance rates among Hispanics are predicted to fall by four percentage points. Nearly all of this change is explained by a reduction in the rate of regional four-year college attendance, which is predicted to fall by an equal amount. In contrast to steady attendance rates among Hispanics, the share of college attenders among non-Hispanic blacks will fall by a few percentage points. Though the dip will be somewhat more pronounced in the Midwest region, the downward drift is predicted in all subregions of the county and across nearly all institution types. Only attendance rates at national and elite colleges will defy the negative trend.

It is unsurprising that the HEDI generally predicts small changes within racial/ethnic groups. Recall that the predicted changes in college attendance shown in table 9.1 are, by construction, driven only by anticipated changes to correlations between race/ethnicity and geographic location, parent education, family composition, sex, and family income. Thus the modest changes predicted in college-going among Hispanics and non-Hispanic blacks and whites might be articulated this way: because the data point to little change in correlations of the demographic variables indicated above over the next 15 years, we have no reason to expect notable changes in college-going. Distributions of factors such as parent education and family income rarely exhibit abrupt changes, and so unless the economy produces large changes in the incentive to go to college, we must usually expect small changes in college attendance rates within population subgroups.

This fact makes forecasted changes among Asian Americans all the more remarkable. The HEDI predicts a five-percentage-point increase in college attendance rates in this already-well-educated subgroup. These gains are expected to be spread more or less evenly across regions of the country, with attendance rates among Asian Americans rising between 4.3 percentage points in the South and 5.0 points in the West and Northeast. As a result, absent other economic or policy innovations, racial/ethnic differences in college attendance rates will increase substantially over the next 15 years. According to the HEDI, by the end of the 2020s Asian Americans will attend college at a rate that is 45 percent higher than Hispanics and 55 percent higher than non-Hispanic blacks. While those differences will be somewhat muted in the West and Northeast, where Hispanics and non-Hispanic blacks have higher matriculation rates, the trend is expected to be experienced more or less equally in all regions.

While the increasing advantage in Asian American educational acquisition is expected to be common to all regions, changes will be markedly different across institution types. By the end of the 2020s, the HEDI forecasts that 28 percent of Asian Americans will attend a two-year college, the same share as in the present. However, attendance rates at regional four-year colleges and universities will increase by more than three percentage points, and the rate of matriculation to national and elite institutions is expected to rise by 10 points. This increase is particularly striking because Asian Americans already attend top intuitions at a rate far surpassing that of other racial/ethnic groups. As a result, at the end of the 2020s their rate of attendance at these schools will top that of non-Hispanic whites by nearly 20 percentage points (33 percent versus 14 percent). Compared with Hispanics and non-Hispanic blacks, Asian Americans' attendance rates at top colleges and universities will be approximately six and eight times as large, respectively.

As in earlier discussions, forecasts related to attendance at selective institutions must be viewed with some caution. That a student has the demographic markers of an elite college student is one thing. Gaining admission is another. If elite colleges and universities admitted all qualified students, over the next 15 years the HEDI predicts that class sizes at these schools would rise by 14 percent and the share of those students who are Asian American would increase from 13 percent to 20 percent. Both of these predictions seem unlikely. In particular, elite schools are likely to respond to rising demand by increasing selectivity. As they do so, they may opt to pass on some highly attractive Asian American students for the sake of a more representative student body. While the Supreme Court ruled in *Grutter v. Bollinger et al.* (2003) and *Fisher v. University of Texas* (2013) that schools cannot use race alone in admission decisions, the benefits of diversity may be used to justify consideration of race/ethnicity among other factors when selecting a class. Such diversity-driven admissions decisions may lead to smaller-than-predicted increases in Asian American attendance rates at elite schools. Still, the forecasts in table 9.1 are unlikely to be too far off the mark on account of these admissions decisions, as Asian Americans passed up by elite schools would almost surely be snatched up by national schools facing decreasing total enrollments.

College Attendance within Family Income Subgroups

Next, we turn to analysis of attendance by family income. The Education Longitudinal Study (ELS) data used to estimate college-going probabilities reports family income only by brackets. In this discussion, high-income families will be defined as those with incomes falling within the top eighth of the income distribution. For the sake of brevity, families whose incomes fall short of this threshold will be termed *low-income*. To put this income threshold in context, among the high school sophomores in the 2002 ELS, the top eighth of the income distribution included families earning $100,000 or more. Adjusting for inflation, that corresponds to approximately $130,000 today.

Chapter 2 notes the strong connection between current college attendance rates and family income observed in the ELS. As seen in the upper panel of table 9.2, this relationship naturally flows through to HEDI forecasts of students in the current college-going generation. Children from high-income families attend college of any kind at an 80 percent clip as compared to a 55 percent matriculation rate among children of less well-off families. These patterns are seen in all four census regions, with slightly lower attendance rates found in the South for both high- and low-income families.

Not surprisingly, the income gap in college attendance is driven by patterns at four-year institutions; two-year-college attendance rates are largely independent of family income. Also predictably, the gap is wider at more selective four-year schools than at regional institutions. While high-income children are 17 percentage points (or 63 percent) more likely to attend a regional four-year institution, they are 10 percentage points (or three times) more likely to attend a national or elite school. While the levels of postsecondary enrollment vary across regions, these attendance advantages never differ by more than one or two percentage points.

The lower panel of table 9.2 uses HEDI forecasts to look ahead to the next 15 years and what may happen to the attendance gap between high- and lower-to-middle-income families. In general, the model projects no substantial changes. Indeed, the model anticipates little change in the rates of postsecondary uptake in either income group. This means that the correlations between family income and other college-going predictors are expected to remain stable or move in

Table 9.2   Forecasted college attendance rates among family income subpopulations by institution type and census region, 2013 and 2028

Type	Family income*	Nation (%)	West (%)	Midwest (%)	Northeast (%)	South (%)
				2013		
Any	Not high income	55	56	57	59	51
	High income	80	80	81	82	77
2-year	Not high income	29	35	30	23	27
	High income	30	36	31	24	29
Regional	Not high income	27	23	28	33	27
4-year	High income	44	39	46	49	45
National/	Not high income	5	3	6	6	4
elite	High income	15	11	17	17	14
				2028		
Any	Not high income	53	56	52	55	50
	High income	77	78	78	78	75
2-year	Not high income	28	33	28	23	26
	High income	31	36	32	25	30
Regional	Not high income	25	23	25	30	25
4-year	High income	42	38	43	47	43
National/	Not high income	4	4	5	5	4
elite	High income	13	11	14	15	12

* High income is defined as being in the top 13 percent of the income distribution among families with a child of a given age (equivalent to $100,000 in the 2002 ELS).

offsetting directions, such that attendance rates within family income groups and the gaps between those rates in the late 2020s will approximate those of today. This is true for all institution types and in all four census regions of the country. Thus whatever problems people perceive today that are associated with income inequality in educational acquisition are likely to be persistent unless some outside force disturbs the system.

College Attendance within Parental Education Subgroups

Finally, we look at attendance rates within groups defined by parental income. Just as in the case of family income, chapter 2 documented wide variation in rates of college attendance across students whose parents differ in educational attainment. These current differences are evident in the upper panel of table 9.3. While children with no parental model of a four-year degree are slightly more likely than not (55 percent) to attend some college, having one parent with a bachelor's degree increases the probability of attendance by 25 percentage points. Having a second parent with a BA adds an additional 10 points, raising the probability of attendance to 90 percent. None of these differences are explained by differential rates of two-year-college matriculation. In fact, children

Table 9.3   Forecasted college attendance rates among parental education subpopulations by institution type and census region, 2013 and 2028

Type	Parent education	Nation (%)	West (%)	Midwest (%)	North-east (%)	South (%)
				2013		
Any	No BA	55	56	57	59	51
	One BA	80	80	81	82	77
	Both BA	90	90	91	91	89
2-year	No BA	29	35	30	23	27
	One BA	30	36	31	24	29
	Both BA	25	29	26	19	25
Regional 4-year	No BA	27	23	28	33	27
	One BA	44	39	46	49	45
	Both BA	53	46	55	57	53
National/elite	No BA	5	3	6	6	4
	One BA	15	11	17	17	14
	Both BA	33	29	34	42	30
				2028		
Any	No BA	53	56	52	55	50
	One BA	77	78	78	78	75
	Both BA	88	88	89	88	87
2-year	No BA	28	33	28	23	26
	One BA	31	36	32	25	30
	Both BA	25	29	26	20	24
Regional 4-year	No BA	25	23	25	30	25
	One BA	42	38	43	47	43
	Both BA	52	46	54	56	52
National/elite	No BA	4	4	5	5	4
	One BA	13	11	14	15	12
	Both BA	32	29	33	39	31

of more educated parents are less likely to attend a two-year program. Attendance at four-year colleges and universities, by contrast, is strongly associated with parent education. Those whose parents both hold a bachelor's degree are about twice as likely to attend a regional four-year institution as are first-generation students. While such an enrollment advantage is sizable, it pales in comparison with that found at national and elite schools, where attendance rates among two-BA progeny are six times as high as those for first-generation students. As in the case of family income, while levels of attendance vary by region, the gaps associated with family background are nearly identical in all areas of the country.

Looking forward 15 years, HEDI forecasts suggest very little change in any of these differences. Anticipated attendance rates for all parental education subgroups, which are reported in the lower panel of table 9.3, are anticipated to remain largely unchanged, such that the gaps between groups are unaffected as well. While the changes are slight, the model predicts lower rates of attendance in all three groups. Approximately half of the predicted changes stem from trends in demographic factors other than parental education. The remaining change is caused by compositional effects described earlier in this chapter. While none of the predicted changes are large in the context of the history shown earlier in this chapter, the HEDI does forecast small reductions in the rate of college attendance by students whose parents hold no or only one four-year degree. In the former group, lower attendance rates are predicted in both two-year and regional four-year institutions. By contrast, lower anticipated attendance among children of one-BA families is entirely due to reductions in four-year college-going. These patterns are precisely what we would expect due to anticipated compositional changes as more and more parents acquire greater and greater education. By the end of the forecast horizon, students without a BA role model will be quite uncommon. Because that circumstance will be even more unusual than it is today, it carries a stronger signal about the families and students who are in this group. As a result, we would not be surprised to see college-going rates in this subgroup dip, as predicted by the model.

At the other end of the parent education spectrum, as more parents acquire a bachelor's degree, the signal of having done so will mean somewhat less in 2028 than it does today. As a result, among students who have only one parental BA role model, we might not be surprised to see four-year attendance rates fall at the same time that a larger share of these students attend two-year colleges. In total, the HEDI predicts very little change in the college-going rates of parent education subpopulations. What differences do exist in the forecasts are largely artifacts of composition effects resulting from the increasing proportion of parents who have earned college degrees in recent years.

A Matter of Policy

The relatively stable HEDI predictions reported previously are in some sense unsurprising: if we continue under the same systems in the future as in the past, then we can expect little change. Overall attendance rates will lag behind projections for our economy's needs, and large gaps across groups will persist or even grow. Of course, it might have been hoped that one or more of the demographic changes under way (particularly the rise in parental education) would have led to a rise in overall attendance rates or a lessening of educational inequalities without policy action on our part. That is not an entirely unreasonable hope—it simply doesn't seem to be supported by evidence. If a free lunch isn't coming our way, then it is reasonable to ask what policies might affect educational attainment gaps and how much progress we might hope to achieve as a result. The next chapter examines academic studies for policy ideas, and then uses the HEDI to quantify the potential for policy innovation to change predictions for the future.

Chapter Ten

The Potential for Policy to Affect Attendance Rates

O n the heels of the Great Recession, economic and educational inequalities have received greater attention in academic, policy, and media discussions. Interest in inequality is hardly surprising given the differences in educational attainment across race/ethnicity, family income, and parent education documented in chapter 9. Higher Education Demand Index forecasts in chapter 9 suggest that we should not count on exogenous increases in overall attendance rates or on a reduction in educational gaps across groups; demographic change and time, on their own, will not cure what ails us. Thankfully, the HEDI is only a forecast model and not a seer. It takes, as given, the patterns of today, and then simply traces out the consequences of demographic change within that context. Policymakers have a real, if partial, ability to change the predicted course through policy innovations. Indeed, much of the new attention to educational inequalities is driven by a desire to adopt new policies that effect change.

To organize the discussion, proposed policy changes will be divided into two broad categories: those that improve student preparation for college work and those that reduce higher education prices paid by families and students. Proposals of both types have been debated and adopted recently. For instance, the omnibus budget bill passed in December 2015 included the Every Student Succeeds Act, which aims to improve K–12 education through a reduction in testing and federal regulation associated with No Child Left Behind. If successful in meeting its goals, this legislation will help states close primary and secondary school preparation gaps, which should, in turn, reduce the differences in postsecondary achievement documented in chapter 9. The omnibus bill also included a permanent extension of American Opportunity tax credits. Because they are means tested, these credits are designed to mitigate attendance gaps by reducing net tuition costs.

Judging by policy statements of 2016 presidential contenders, additional reforms may follow.[1] To better prepare students for college, leading candidates have proposed expanding pre-K education funding, increasing school choice, reforming the Common Core, improving college counseling and other sources of college search information, and simplifying the application for federal financial aid.[2] Even as they paid close attention to better preparation for college, candidates also foreshadowed policy change regarding college financing. Proposals to reduce the net price of higher education include: reducing interest rates on student loans, increasing the college expense tax deduction, and expanding aid to the states to incentivize greater higher education investments such that in-state students graduate debt free or attend with no tuition costs.[3] (The details of so-called zero tuition proposals vary with some targeting community colleges only and others including four-year institutions as well.)

The intuitive arguments behind both college readiness and college cost initiatives are clear enough. However, a brief detour into economic theory is worthwhile here because public investments in education may arguably violate the general rule that we must choose between greater equality and more efficiency. Okun (1975) articulated this broad principle in his aptly titled book *Equality and Efficiency: The Big Tradeoff*. In broad analyses of fiscal policy, economists have disagreed about the severity of the trade-off, but debate participants generally accept the premise: if we want more equal outcomes, we must accept a smaller "size of the pie." (See Allgood and Snow 1998, Ballard 1988, and Browning and Johnson 1984 for several important contributions to this discussion.) Education investments may be one instance in which we can have our pie and eat it, too. This possibility can be understood using the supply and demand framework proposed in Becker and Tomes (1979 and 1986). In this widely employed model, parents make educational investments in their children by comparing the cost with the benefit. The opportunity cost of the investment is determined by the interest rate, which acts as a price for money. The primary benefit of education is that it expands the child's life opportunities and increases wages. Becker and Tomes reasonably assume that the benefits of education are higher for more-able children. Because this is so, high-ability kids are more likely to attend college.

Genetic and social heritability of ability produces a positive correlation between parent and child ability that, in turn, leads to a positive relationship between parent and child educational attainment and earnings.

Having developed this basic framework, Becker and Tomes consider a slightly more complex environment in which borrowing constraints limit parents' abilities to pay for education. In this setting, high-ability children born to parents with lower incomes cannot afford expensive education, even though such an investment might easily pay off in the long run. Despite the high returns on educational investments in such children, banks are unwilling to make educational loans because, unlike a mortgage or business loan, the investment being made with the loan proceeds—the child's human capital—cannot be collateralized. So, in a world without borrowing constraints, we expect "natural" intergenerational inequalities flowing from the positive relationship between parent and child ability. In the presence of a borrowing constraint, inequalities are inefficiently amplified when parents are unable to invest appropriately in their children's schooling. In such an environment, a government program that reduced tuition costs or guaranteed student loans might theoretically be paid for by taxing the next generation's larger earnings while simultaneously reducing educational disparities—a rare equality-efficiency win-win.

Economists do not debate the basic implication of Becker and Tomes's conclusions that laissez-faire policies will likely lead to educational inequalities due to financial constraints that limit student access to education. But the status quo is hardly laissez-faire. In the 2013–14 school year, federal, state, and local governments appropriated more than $600 billion to public elementary and secondary schools (NCES 2016, table 235.10). In addition, state governments spent around $90 billion and the federal government $200 billion on higher education (Mumper et al. 2016, SHEEHO 2016). Given these levels of government intervention, economists do debate the continuing role of financial barriers in perpetuating inequalities under current policies. Do the associations between family income and college attendance seen in chapter 9 follow from a causal connection, or are they merely artifacts of intergenerational correlation of ability? While a detailed review of this literature is beyond the scope of this chapter, interested readers can learn more in an overview by Grawe (2007) or primary studies by Cameron and Heckman (1998, 1999, 2001), Card (1999, 2001), Carneiro and Heckman (2002, 2003), DeLong et al. (2003), Ellwood and Kane (2000), Grawe (2004, 2008), Grawe and Mulligan (2002), Haveman and Smeeding (2006), Kane (1994, 2004), and Krueger (2003).

While researchers disagree about how the income-education correlation should be understood in connection to borrowing constraints, we have reached a good deal of agreement about the magnitude of the effect of net tuition reductions on higher education demand. A $1,000 reduction in net tuition increases attendance rates by approximately three and a half to five percentage points (Abraham and Clark 2006, Kane 2004). Moreover, most researchers find that this effect is larger among underrepresented groups. Specifically, the response of tuition reductions is approximately 50 percent larger for blacks than for whites (Kane 1994). And within the white population, the effect of cost reductions on college attendance found in the bottom quartile of the income distribution (4.6 percentage points per $1,000 net tuition reduction) is almost four times as large as the effect among whites in the top quartile (1.2 points) (Kane 1994). These empirical findings suggest that proposals to reduce college prices may indeed narrow attendance gaps.

Of course, implementation details of tuition reductions can easily reverse the effects so that attendance gaps are increased even as average tuition costs fall. For example, the federal HOPE Scholarship and Lifetime Learning Credit, Coverdell Education Savings Accounts, and state-sponsored 529 plans are available to all but the highest-income families. However, the tax benefits of plans like these are typically correlated with income such that gains are greater for middle- and upper-income families than for low-income peers. For example, Dynarski (2000, 2002) studies the effect of Georgia's HOPE Scholarship, which promises free tuition at Georgia's public colleges to any state resident graduating high school with a B average or better. Qualifying students attending private schools can claim additional grant aid from the state. Dynarski confirms the general effect sizes reported by Kane, estimating that attendance rates rise by about five percentage points for each $1,000 in subsidy. However, she finds that these gains are mostly concentrated among white and upper-income students. Dynarski suspects this regressive outcome follows from two elements of the program design. First, the grade-point requirement excludes larger portions of underrepresented populations. Moreover, because the HOPE scholarship offsets Federal Pell Grants dollar for dollar, it creates little or no net reduction in tuition costs faced by low-income families.

Public efforts to reduce tuition also vary in transparency in ways that may lead to differential rates of effectiveness. For instance, Kane (1994) finds that expansions in Federal Pell Grants are less efficacious than reductions in tuition. He posits that while increasing grant aid by $1 and decreasing the sticker price by $1 have an identical effect on the ultimate net price, the latter is far more visible, and so college attendance may respond more to changes in tuition levels, even if a student's financial situation makes Pell eligibility unquestionable. If Kane's interpretation is correct, then programs that improve college counseling may be useful in raising college attendance among low-income students.

The estimates described above allow us to assess the degree to which tuition reduction policies could increase overall attendance rates and mitigate current gaps. According to the College Board's (2016) report on trends in higher education costs, average net tuition and fees at two-year institutions have not topped $500 since 1998–99 and have been negative for the past four years. This suggests we should expect little effect on attendance rates or enrollment gaps were we to adopt a "free community college" policy; current funding already accomplishes this goal in much of the country.[4] The same College Board study finds that average in-state net tuition at public four-year institutions rose from about $2,000 in 1996–97 to just more than $3,800 in 2016–17. (Note that these figures intentionally exclude the costs of room and board since students must be fed and housed regardless of their education choice.) If attendance rates increase according to Kane's (1994) estimates, a "free four-year college" policy could increase enrollments by 15 to 25 percentage points among low-income blacks, 10 to 15 points among low-income whites, and 5 to 10 points among middle- and high-income whites. When compared with the gaps identified in chapter 9, it seems an aggressive tuition reduction policy could substantially alter college attendance patterns in coming years.

Alternative Futures

Given the evidence described above, it is easy to imagine new or expanded policies targeting attendance gaps along dimensions of family income or race/ethnicity—hypotheticals that the HEDI framework can explore. Because demographic variables are correlated with one another, programs that aim to reduce gaps along one dimension will indirectly affect other gaps at the same time. For example, if a tuition reduction policy increased attendance rates among students from low-income families, we might also expect higher attendance rates among Hispanics and non-Hispanic blacks, who are disproportionately represented among lower-income households. But by how much? The following analysis uses the HEDI model to explore this question.

The first thought experiment examines a world in which the effects of family income are substantially reduced. Specifically, I alter the probit regression coefficients on income in both high school persistence and college attendance, eliminating half of the estimated difference between the highest family income group (i.e., the one with the strongest higher education attachment) and each of the other seven income groups. The policy change being considered here would be substantial. To put it in context, consider how college-going behavior would have been different among those reaching age 18 in the years 2012 through 2014 had income played only half the role it actually did. In this hypothetical world, the fraction of students attending a four-year institution would rise to just more than 50 percent—a 10-point increase from the current rate of 41 percent. At the same time, we would have experienced a five-percentage-point drop in two-year institution attendance, resulting in a net seven-point increase in broad college-going. Clearly, no policy intervention could have an immediate impact like that described here. But it is possible to imagine that an aggressive policy, implemented soon, could halve effects of income for the cohorts entering college in the years 2027 to 2029. Such change would go a long way toward meeting the economy's projected needs for a more highly skilled workforce.

But how would it affect predicted gaps in attendance at two- and four-year institutions? Because income is only slightly correlated with attendance at two-year schools, such a policy change would have little to no effect on gaps at such schools, whether along the dimension of race, parent education, or income. By contrast, policies that leveled the playing field across income groups would notably mitigate gaps in attendance at four-year colleges and universities.[5] The direct effect of such a change on attendance gaps across income groups would be (not surprisingly) quite large. In the counterfactual world in which income plays a smaller role in college attendance decisions, the gap between high- and low-income students in the year 2028 falls by approximately one-quarter, from 38 percentage points to 29 points.[6]

Indirectly, reducing the effects of income will also affect gaps across parent education and race/ethnicity groups. Under the status quo, the four-year college-going gap between Asian Americans and Hispanics is expected to grow from 29 percentage points to 37 points in the next 15 years. If Hispanics, who earn lower incomes on average, attended college at a higher rate due to a reduction in income effects, the resulting gap would be reduced by one-fifth, to 29 points, eliminating (though not reversing) this negative trend. Differences between Asians and non-Hispanic blacks would also be reduced from 35 percentage points under the status quo to 32 points in the counterfactual, a 10 percent reduction. While this still means non-Hispanic blacks will lose ground to Asian Americans, the loss would be smaller if income played a smaller role in college attendance decisions.

In a similar way, reducing income effects would diminish college-going differences across parent education groups. Under the status quo, these gaps are expected to hold steady, with children from families with no parental bachelor's almost 50 percentage points less likely to attend college throughout the next 15 years. A policy that halved income effects would reduce this gap to 42 points. It is interesting to note that a policy that reduced income effects would remove a larger share of the gap between one- and two-BA families than between zero- and two-BA families. That is, income plays a bigger role in the smaller of the two gaps. By contrast, reducing income effects had the biggest effect on the largest of the race/ethnicity gaps (Hispanics vs. Asian Americans). So, in one dimension attending to the disadvantages of income would benefit those in the most disadvantaged group but not so in the other.

In a second thought experiment, the effects of race/ethnicity are halved. Since Asian Americans have the greatest degree of educational uptake, the hypothetical policy alters all race/ethnicity model coefficients one-half of the way from their estimated values to those of Asian Americans. Again, the extent of the imagined policy change can be measured by considering how overall college-going behavior would have been different among those reaching age 18 in the years 2012 through 2014 had effects of race/ethnicity been lower than current levels. If attendance patterns of other racial/ethnic groups looked more like those of Asian Americans, the fraction of students attending a four-year institution would rise from the current rate of 41 percent to 48 percent. Rates of two-year college attendance would be more or less unchanged, increasing by two points, resulting in a net six-point increase in broad college-going had differences across race/ethnicity been half the size they currently are. These effect sizes are only slightly smaller than those of halving income effects and would similarly do much to address the economy's need for a more-educated labor force.

While leading to similar effects on overall attendance rates, a race/ethnicity-targeted intervention would be less effective in mitigating gaps experienced by underrepresented groups. As in the first experiment, which relaxed effects of income when direct effects of race/ethnicity are reduced, the greatest impact is found in four-year college-going patterns. The direct effect would be to cut race/ethnicity gaps across groups by approximately one-quarter relative to the status quo. Where the HEDI predicts that the Hispanic–Asian American gap would increase from 29 percentage points to 37 points under the status quo, a policy that halved race/ethnicity effects would hold that gap constant. Similarly, the expected status quo increase in the disadvantage for non-Hispanic blacks—from 25 percentage points to 35 points—would be all but neutralized. The ultimate effect on race/ethnicity gaps is similar to that found in the previous income-targeting hypothetical policy change.

Despite this resemblance, a policy directed at gaps across race/ethnicity would have only modest indirect effects on other dimensions of disadvantage. Gaps between high- and low-income groups would fall only marginally, from 38 percentage points today to 36 points in 2028, under this hypothetical policy. Similarly, the gap between children with zero and two parental BA role models would fall only from 48 percentage points today to 45 in the late 2020s if we were to find a way to diminish the effects of race/ethnicity. In all, a policy targeting race/ethnicity would have more focused impacts than one targeting the effects of income.

Big-Picture Lessons

Stepping back from the specifics of these two thought experiments, the patterns just described point to several important policy implications. First, it is possible to imagine alternative worlds; the forecasts in previous chapters are hardly written in stone. Attendance gaps between Asian Americans and other groups need not explode. Differences across income groups need not persist decades ahead. While a vigorous debate should precede policy change, findings in the economics literature combined with the HEDI framework show that if we decide the benefits of such change outweigh the costs, we can halt and even reverse these trends.

Second, while the economy's needs for greater educational attainment are substantially higher than we have achieved in recent years, it is possible to imagine plausible policy interventions that could hope to make significant progress on this front. In fact, both thought experiments produced significantly higher college attendance rates. Perhaps this is unsurprising since the problem of low attendance rates is reduced anytime a new student enrolls (regardless of their demographic profile), while gaps across groups are only addressed when particular students enroll. Still, the thought experiments produce impressive overall gains—a nearly 25 percent increase in attendance rates—using policies that, while aggressive, are plausible both politically and economically.

Third, by comparing the two counterfactual worlds we see that some policies have broader potential to mitigate college attendance gaps than others. In particular, a policy that mitigates income effects is more likely to also reduce gaps in other dimensions, while a policy directed toward differences by race/ethnicity would have only modest effects beyond the direct target. This finding is perhaps convenient in that policies explicitly targeting race/ethnicity raise a host of philosophical and legal questions. By contrast, we have a long history of providing means-tested aid. Expansion of aid to low-income families could be used to diminish gaps in other dimensions without confronting those more difficult questions.

Finally, results of the thought experiments underscore the limitations of policy. For example, despite the large interventions imagined, neither hypothetical policy reduced the expected growth in race/ethnicity gaps. While most of the growth in the gap is accounted for by increased attendance rates among Asian Americans rather than decreasing rates among other groups, to the degree that societal welfare depends on relative rather than absolute status, coming demographic shifts will create increased concerns around equity in twenty-first-century education. Aggressively targeting income can mitigate the problem—but three-quarters of today's gap would remain even after an aggressive policy intervention. This is perhaps the most important and sobering lesson from the counterfactual analysis: demographic changes already in motion foreshadow race/ethnicity, family income, and parental education attendance gaps so large that even aggressive policy interventions are unlikely to eliminate them in the mid-term future. Instead, we must accept that this challenge will require sustained attention.

Chapter Eleven

Looking beyond 2030

Because they are based on observed children in the 2011 American Community Survey, the Higher Education Demand Index forecasts are inherently limited to extend no further than 2029, when the youngest children in the survey reach college-going age. In a literal sense, nothing can be ruled out in the years 2030 and beyond. That is unfortunate because while the resulting estimates provide plenty for higher education administrators to think about over the next decade, some strategies for handling coming demographic change may make more or less sense depending on what we think will happen beyond the model's forecast horizon. By looking at the most recent data releases, we can already anticipate some features of higher education demand in the early 2030s. At least as importantly, it is possible to identify several critical demographic variables that should be carefully watched as leading indicators of the future that extends beyond the model forecast period.

The first and most obvious metric to watch is the total fertility rate. While it is critical to adjust for the probability of college attendance to understand impacts of more nuanced demographic change, demand at two-year and regional four-year institutions closely follow population. When, if ever, will the fertility rate rebound? The most recent *National Vital Statistics Report* from the Centers for Disease Control and Prevention (CDC; 2017) suggests we may not yet have found the bottom. After a miniscule rise of one-quarter of one percent in 2014, in 2015 the total fertility rate continued its downward trajectory—off another one percent. This provides little hope for a recovery in enrollment levels through at least 2033. Still, what happens next could be critically important to institutions as they confront the leading edge of the birth dearth in 2026. A rebound in fertility rates by 2017 might allow schools with steady enrollment through the mid-2020s to cope with the subsequent dip with temporizing measures. This may be particularly true of second-tier schools whose enrollments aren't projected to fall short of present levels until 2029. Alternatively, if birth rates remain low through 2020 or longer, there will be little benefit in delaying inevitable adjustments.

Those same CDC reports divide fertility rates between demographic groups. These breakdowns can hint at how the probability of college-going may change with time. For example, as the economic recovery reaches completion, the Hispanic fertility rate may revert to higher levels prevalent before the Great Recession. Conversely, higher college attendance rates in this population may create pressure for continued convergence in fertility rates across race/ethnicity groups. These trends will determine the degree to which the race/ethnicity distribution continues to shift toward Hispanics (and the geographic distribution toward the Southwest) beyond 2030.

Similarly, birth rates by age of mother are quite revealing. The 2014 uptick in fertility was driven by an acceleration in the tilt toward fertility after age 30. Perhaps this reflects the first fruits of delayed fertility stemming from the financial crisis. As a result, not only are there more kids in the high school class of 2032 than in the class of 2031 (though only slightly), but those children are more likely to live with parents with established careers who are in a better position to support college attendance in the future. For this reason (and many others), we would all be glad to see teen birth rates continue the downward trend of the past two-plus decades.

To the extent that the use of high-tuition/high-aid pricing models continues to expand, the financial stability of higher education will become increasingly sensitive to the economic health of the upper-middle class. As shown in chapter 7, real household incomes have been flat across this portion of the income distribution for more than 15 years. Perhaps most worrisome is the near stagnation of incomes at the heart of the distribution; real household incomes at the 40th and 60th percentiles have risen less than 5 and 12 percent, respectively, since 1973. If these trends continue, changes to pricing strategy will offer limited potential to raise significant new revenue—and if some aid-eligible students are so intimidated by high sticker prices that they don't even apply, the policy may create additional enrollment losses.

Of course, the economic health of middle- to upper-income families is strongly affected by the economic returns to higher education. It is no coincidence that Goldin and Katz (2008) find a stagnating college wage premium since 1990—the same time period over which upper-middle-class household incomes have been flat. Given that the current premium stands near historic highs, it is unlikely that we will see a repeat of the 1980s, during which a rising premium induced greater demand that spared higher education the worst effects of a birth dearth. Far from hoping for a renewal of the upward trend, administrators should watch to see if the slight, post-2000 decrease in the college wage premium becomes a deeper, persistent trend. In that case, actual enrollment changes may be far more challenging than HEDI forecasts would suggest.

To the extent that some institutions intend to navigate the demographic shifts through outreach to underrepresented groups, an early and honest look at attendance rates will be important. As described in chapter 9, with the exception of very recent reductions in the Hispanic–white attendance gap, enrollment differences across income, parent education, and race/ethnicity groups have been remarkably persistent. New recruitment strategies or public policies might theoretically achieve levels of equality that have eluded us for decades. But if an institution were to bet its future on that proposition, it would be good to see evidence of that outcome no later than 2020, when it still may be possible to craft a "Plan B."

Finally, George Stigler's (1958) "survival principle" points to an important early indicator of higher education trends: the success of our peers. Writing in the context of a profit-maximizing firm deciding on an optimal scale, Stigler notes that we can often infer the best path forward by observing the choices and outcomes of those who have acted before us. In short, you could do worse than to note which subsectors of your industry are succeeding, and then model your investments to match. Market players following unprofitable strategies go out of business, while those pursuing better tactics come to play a larger role in the industry. Several caveats to this survivor principle obviously come to mind. If the environment has recently changed (or we know it is about to), then designing strategies to mimic yesterday's winners can be a very bad idea. However, even acknowledging those concerns, aping successful peers is a powerful concept.

Applied to coming demographic change, we can imagine examining the successes (and failures) of the institutions that are first to confront enrollment declines. These schools serve as canaries in the coal mine. The current volume's website includes maps and data of HEDI growth forecasts through 2020.[1] These can be used to locate institutions that will involuntarily lead in higher education's response to lagging enrollments. In a crude first pass, in 2020 institutions may look at similar schools recruiting from areas already experiencing what is predicted for their own recruitment pool over the following decade. For example, in 2020 a regional four-year college drawing students primarily from rural Minnesota and Minneapolis–St. Paul may look at peers that recruit in rural Michigan. After all, by 2020 these Michigan peers will be well into a moderate enrollment contraction similar to what the Minnesota institution can anticipate over the subsequent decade.

However, as earlier chapters have emphasized, the best response for any given institution will depend greatly on how other institutions change behavior. The comparison between Michigan and Minnesota breaks down when looking at forecasts for other institution types. By 2020, Michigan enrollments will be down for all institution types. By contrast, between 2020 and 2029, Minnesota promises strong growth among elite college students. National and elite schools facing those Michigan losses may alter their recruitment to poach students from regional schools in the area. By 2020, the regional four-year institution in Michigan may see few choices other than budget cutting, while the Minnesota school in the mid-2020s may successfully target students who would have otherwise attended better colleges and universities in the past. In all, strategies seen to be successful in the Michigan context of 2020 may not serve regional four-year institutions in Minnesota very well in the subsequent decade. As it turns out, participants in the San Antonio market may be more useful guides to this Minnesota school; by 2020, that market will see moderate losses in two-year and regional four-year students, steep reductions in national students, and strong growth in elite students—the same pattern as expected for Minnesota a decade later. Of course, other factors also dictate how "peers" should be defined, but a good place to start is to find other schools that have already successfully navigated the problems of your future.

The next 15 years will present serious challenges to much of higher education as demographic shifts already under way are further complicated by a new birth dearth. As true as this may be, it must be recognized that change is ever present and every generation has faced challenges of its own—the Vietnam War and social change in the 1960s, economic challenges of the 1970s and 1980s, diversification of the student body in the 1990s, and the financial crisis of the 2000s. What is different about the coming demographic change is that we can see it coming from a distance and can plan ahead. Armed with the right data and careful analysis, we can adapt to ensure that institutions of higher education continue to meet their individual and societal missions.

Methodological Appendix

Section 1: The Model

The forecasted demand for higher education is a probability-weighted average of projected headcounts. More formally, the expected demand for college of institutional type j from state or metropolitan locality l in year t (denoted as D_{jlt}) is given by

$$D_{jlt} = \Sigma_{s,r,d,i,e_m,e_f,y,f} P_j(s,r,d,b,e_m,e_f,y,f) * N_{18lt}(s,r,d,b,e_m,e_f,y,f) \tag{1}$$

where $P_j(.)$ is the probability that someone of a given demographic type achieves outcome j, $N_{18lt}(.)$ is the number of 18-year-olds of that demographic profile living in locality l in cohort t, s is sex, r is race/ethnicity, d captures census division and urban/rural residence status, b indicates whether native-born, e_m is mother's education, e_f is father's education, y is family income, and f is family structure. The Higher Education Demand Index (HEDI) uses estimates of $P_j(.)$ generated from the restricted portion of the 2002 Education Longitudinal Study (ELS), which tracks educational choices made by a representative sample of 16,197 high school students who were sophomores in the year 2002. Section 2 of this appendix describes how each of these demographic categories is defined in the data and the estimation of $P_j(.)$.

The number of 18-year-old children of a given demographic type living in each location in a given year in the future is estimated based on the number of children aged 0 to 17 reported (using person weights) in the 2011 American Community Survey (ACS). A crude population forecast model assumes that the number of children from each birth cohort (observed when a years old) in a locality l remains constant over time:

$$N_{18lt}(.) = N_{alt-(18-a)}(.). \tag{2}$$

For example, if the New York metropolitan area was home to 10,000 12-year-olds with a given demographic profile in 2011, then a simplistic approach might predict that there will be 10,000 18-year-olds fitting that same demographic profile in the New York metropolitan area in 2017. Substituting equation (2) into equation (1) yields the baseline forecast model:

$$D_{jlt+(18-a)} = \Sigma_{s,r,d,i,e_m,e_f,y,f} P_j(s,r,d,b,e_m,e_f,y,f) * N_{alt}(s,r,d,b,e_m,e_f,y,f) \tag{3}$$

While chapter 3 demonstrates that this baseline model does a reasonable job of forecasting aggregate state and metropolitan populations, it rests on several strong assumptions that may be important when considering subpopulations. Specifically, the baseline model assumes the following:

- *An individual's demographic characteristics don't change over time.* While it may be sensible to assume time invariance of sex, race/ethnicity, and (for the most part) parents' educational attainment, evidence in section 3 suggests that more than 20 percent of children in the ACS will experience a change in family structure between the point of observation and age 18.
- *No one drops out of high school prior to the sophomore year.* (The design of the ELS inherently misses children who leave school before tenth grade.)
- *Children do not migrate between states/metropolitan localities.*
- *All children live to age 18.*
- *There is no immigration into birth cohorts between observation in the ACS and age 18.*

The remainder of this section briefly explains how the baseline model is modified to relax these assumptions. Later sections provide additional detail.

Change in Family Structure

Using data from the Panel Study of Income Dynamics, I estimate the probability of moving from one family structure to another conditional on mother's education. The estimated probability that a child of a given demographic type will attend a college of type j is defined as the weighted average of four college-going probabilities— one for each of four family structures (living with both parents, with mother alone, with father alone, or with neither parent)—using the estimated probabilities of family structure change as weights. To account for the correlation between income and number of parents in the household, college-going probabilities are adjusted to reflect a revised income measure that captures expected gains and losses in family income observed when family structures change. Let y' denote the ultimate family income bracket following adjustment for changes in family structure. For a child observed at age a living in family structure f who may end up in one of four ultimate family structures f', the resulting probability of attending a school of type j is given by

$$P_j(s,r,d,b,e_m,e_f,y,f) = \Sigma_{f'} F_{f \to f'}(e_m,a) * P_j(s,r,d,b,e_m,e_f,y',f')$$

Where $F_{f \to f'}(e_m, a)$ is the probability of a transition from family structure f to f', which is dependent on mother's education and the child's age.

Incorporating this modification into equation (3)

$$D_{jlt+(18-a)} = \Sigma_{s,r,d,i,e_m,e_f,y,f} [\Sigma_{f'} F_{f \to f'}(e_m,a) * P_j(s,r,d,b,e_m,e_f,y',f')] \qquad (4)$$
$$* N_{alt}(s,r,d,b,e_m,e_f,y,f).$$

Detailed descriptions of the estimates of $F_{f \to f'}(e_m, a)$ and adjustments to family income are provided in section 3.

Retention to Sophomore Year of High School

The probabilities of attending college are estimated on the ELS sample of high school sophomores. While nearly all children remain in school until the sophomore year due to truancy laws, some students reach the minimum school-leaving age before the timing of the ELS sample. (In the ACS, 5 percent of 16-year-olds report not attending school.) To account for school completion before the ELS sampling window, the HEDI estimates the probability of retention until the sophomore year R conditional on demographic characteristics making an adjustment for change in family structure analogous to that for the probability of college-going described previously:

$$R(s,r,d,b,e_m,e_f,y,f) = \Sigma_{f'} F_{f \to f'}(e_m,a) * R(s,r,d,b,e_m,e_f,y',f')$$

Incorporating this adjustment into equation (4),

$$D_{jlt+(18-a)} = \Sigma_{s,r,d,i,e_m,e_f,y,f} [\Sigma_{f'} F_{f \to f'}(e_m,a) * P_j(s,r,d,b,e_m,e_f,y',f')] \tag{5}$$
$$* R(s,r,d,b,e_m,e_f,y,f) * N_{alt}(s,r,d,b,e_m,e_f,y,f).$$

Section 4 describes the estimation of school retention probabilities based on data from the ACS.

Migration between States/Metropolitan Areas

In the 2011 ACS, more than 2 percent of children live in families that report a different location of residence than that of the previous year (where locations are defined as described in chapter 3). To account for moves by native-born children between the time of observation in the ACS and age 18, I estimate transition matrices for movements between 63 cities and nonmetropolitan portions of states.[1] These migration matrices T are estimated separately conditional on the child's age a, mother's education e_m, and race/ethnicity r. Section 5 gives a detailed description of the process for estimating these transition matrices.

Given the estimated probability that a child observed in locality l_o will be in locality l at age 18 (element l_o, l of $T(a,e_m,r)$), I calculate the expected number of children of each demographic type in each locality l at age 18:

$$N_{alt}(s,r,d,b,e_m,e_f,y,f) = \Sigma_{l_o} T_{l_o l}(a,e_m,r) N_{al_o t}(s,r,d,b,e_m,e_f,y,f).$$

Migration from locality l_o to locality l also changes the probability of attending a college of type j if the locations differ in census division and/or urban/rural status d. Let the associated marginal change in the probability implied by $P_j(s, r, d, i, e_m, e_f, y, f)$ be called $\Delta P_j(d, d')$ where d and d' correspond to localities l_o and l, respectively.[2] (If, for a given observation the resulting adjusted probability is less than zero, the probability of achieving outcome j is set to zero for that observation.) Revising equation (6) to calculate the expected number of children in each state, controlling for movements between states/metropolitan areas and resulting changes in the probability of college-going:

$$D_{jlt+(18-a)} = \Sigma_{s,r,d,b,e_m,e_f,y,f}[\Sigma_{f'}F_{f\to f'}(e_m,a)*P_j(s,r,d,b,e_m,e_f,y',f')] \tag{6}$$
$$*[R(s,r,d,b,e_m,e_f,y,f)+\Delta P_j(d,d')]$$
$$*[\Sigma_{l_o}T_{l_o l}(a,e_m,r)*N_{al_o t}(s,r,d,b,e_m,e_f,y,f)].$$

Mortality and Immigration

Each native child younger than age 18 represents slightly less than one child at the time of college-going due to mortality in the intervening years.[3] Section 6 describes how mortality tables from the Centers for Disease Control and Prevention (CDC) form estimates of survival conditional on age and race/ethnicity.

While cohort size among native children only diminishes with time, the number of nonnative children in a cohort and state/metropolitan area can either increase or decrease with time. First, a small fraction of nonnative children die. Second, nonnative families who are already here (and so in the ACS sample) migrate around the country. Finally, new families arrive with nonnative children who are not counted in the ACS.

Section 7 describes adjustments to account simultaneously for inflows to and movements of the foreign-born population. Making the assumption that mortality, migration, and immigration continue to follow existing patterns, the HEDI uses within state/city estimates of the relationship between age and foreign-born cohort sizes to create a scaling variable that is applied to observed counts of nonnatives to estimate the number of such children who will be 18 in any given year.

Corrections for mortality among the native-born and mortality, migration, and immigration among nonnatives are essentially identical: a child observed in a cohort today represents more or less than one child in the year that that cohort reaches age 18. A scaling variable $S(a,r,d,b)$ varies by age and (depending on whether the individual was born in the United States) race/ethnicity, census division, and foreign-born status. Applying this scaling variable to headcounts in the ACS, equation (6) is revised:

$$D_{jlt+(18-a)} = \Sigma_{s,r,d,b,e_m,e_f,y,f}[[\Sigma_{f'}F_{f\to f'}(e_m,a)*P_j(s,r,d,b,e_m,e_f,y',f')] \tag{7}$$
$$*R(s,r,d,b,e_m,e_f,y,f)+\Delta P_j(d,d')]*\Sigma_{l_o} T_{l_o l}(a,edf,y)$$
$$*S(a,r,d,b)*N_{al_o t}(s,r,d,b,e_m,e_f,y,f).$$

Equation (7) represents the full forecast model.

Section 2: Estimating the Probability of College-Going

The HEDI model estimates college-going probabilities from a logistic regression analysis of data from the 2002 ELS. Because coefficients from these models are applied to headcounts in the ACS, all predictors must have close equivalents in the ACS dataset. Briefly, the variables available in both datasets include:

- Sex: male or female
- Race/ethnicity: Non-Hispanic white, non-Hispanic black, Hispanic, Asian, or other

- Sex-race/ethnicity interaction
- Mother's education and father's education: no diploma, high school, some college, four-year degree, or more than four-year degree
- Urbanicity: Whether living in a metropolitan statistical area with population two million or greater
- Census division
- Family income (in eight brackets)

The model divides ELS data into five subgroups:

1. Native-born children living with both parents
2. Native-born children living with mother only
3. Native-born children living with father only
4. Native-born children living with neither mother nor father
5. Foreign-born children

Small subsample sizes in the ELS (particularly for the last three categories) and the absence of parent education observations for those living with neither parent necessitate the following simplifications to the full model just described:

- When children live with mother only
  o Exclude father's education
- When children live with father only
  o Exclude ethnicity and its interaction with sex
  o Exclude mother's education
  o Collapse father's education into two categories: more than four-year degree and other
  o Collapse census divisions into census regions
  o Collapse family income into five brackets by combining brackets 1 to 4 and 7 to 8
- When children live with neither parent or are foreign-born
  o Make all of the simplifications noted for children living with father only
  o Exclude father's education

To account for the original ELS sampling scheme along with attrition between the initial 2002 survey and the ELS follow-up survey, regressions are weighted using the ELS-constructed weighting variable F2BYWT, the second follow-up base year panel weight.

The remainder of this section gives descriptions of variable definitions. Supplemental materials available on the book website provide additional detail on how categories of variables were assigned in the two datasets to achieve the closest correspondence.[4] To assess the comparability of the crosswalk between the data sources, the material that follows also compares distributions of the exogenous variables in the 2002 ELS with those for 16-year-olds in the 2000 Census. (The census uses the same variable categories as the 2011 ACS.[5])

Definitions of Independent Variables
Demographic Variables

The crosswalks between the ELS and ACS for observations of sex, race/ethnicity, and parent education are relatively straightforward. By contrast, the coding for family composition involves several judgment calls because the ELS provides a rich set of family structure options, while the ACS does not. In fact, the latter includes no explicit measure of family composition, and so composition is inferred by reports of parental education that imply presence of the parent in the household. The ultimate crosswalk was chosen to best align the family composition distributions in the ELS (using the base year student weights) and the 2000 Census. Even the best-fitting coding scheme results in some differences in the two distributions. Most notably, the 2002 ELS includes a slightly greater proportion of children living with both mother and father (73 percent as compared with 65 percent in the ACS), with more or less equal reductions in the other three family structures.

The ELS records incomes by bracket in the variable BYINCOME; the ACS records family income (FTOTINC) in dollars. While it is possible to assign approximate income levels to ELS income brackets, and then adjust for inflation between 2002 and 2011, this approach to reconciling the datasets raises questions of comparability across children of different ages whose parents are also at different points in the life cycle. Specifically, young children in the ACS are likely to live in families with lower absolute incomes because their parents are at the start of their careers. It is easy to imagine a family with modest absolute income still ranking very highly in the income distribution of the subset of families with a very young child. In this case, a measure of absolute income would spuriously suggest that family incomes of college-going children will be lower 15 years from now than they are today. As a result, the crosswalk recodes ACS income observations to reflect the position (percentile) of the child's family income within the distribution of all families with a child of that age. For tractability, ELS family income groups are collapsed into the following eight categories (percentage of ELS sample given in parentheses):

- None, $1,000–$15,000 (10 percent)
- $15,001–$25,000 (12 percent)
- $25,001–$35,000 (12 percent)
- $35,001–$50,000 (20 percent)
- $50,001–$75,000 (21 percent)
- $75,001–$100,000 (13 percent)
- $100,000–$200,000 (10 percent)
- $200,001 or more (3 percent)

Using the aforementioned percentiles to define cutoffs in the ACS data, ACS observations are similarly categorized into eight income brackets. (For example, the lowest income bracket corresponds to the lowest 10 percent, the second bracket corresponds to the next lowest 12 percent, and so on.) One complication arises among ACS children living with neither mother nor father. In this subset, a little more than one-quarter of the children report no family income observation. Using the other three-quarters of observations for whom income is reported, the model imputes family income by regressing observed family income on race/ethnicity, location, age, and age-squared.

Geographic Variables

The HEDI divides the country into metropolitan statistical areas (MSAs) and residual, nonmetropolitan portions of states to create 63 localities with populations no smaller than two million people as measured by the 2011 ACS. When states or nonmetropolitan portions of states have populations below this threshold, contiguous areas are combined within census divisions to create localities with sufficient population. For example, North Dakota, South Dakota, Nebraska, and nonmetropolitan Kansas form a single location. The resulting set of localities includes 28 metropolitan areas and 35 states or nonmetropolitan portions of states.

Neither the ACS nor the ELS record whether respondents live in a particular MSA, however. The former codes observations by public use micro areas (PUMAs). For confidentiality reasons, when coding the location of former residence the ACS uses "PUMAs of migration" (defined by ACS variables MIGPUMA1 and MIGPLAC1), which combine PUMAs when necessary to ensure a minimum population threshold. To allow crosswalking between the two PUMA variables, the ACS provides the variable PUMARES2MIG, which, when combined with the STATEFIP code, indicates the PUMA of migration in which the individual currently resides. Using this variable, it is possible to calculate the fraction of people in a PUMA of migration who live in each PUMA of residence. I assume all of those who lived in a given PUMA of migration lived in the PUMA of residence accounting for the greatest fraction of residents in that PUMA of migration. I then use the Missouri Census Data Center webtool to match PUMAs of residence to MSAs.[6]

The ELS reports the census division (BYCENDIV) and zip code (BYSCHZIP) of each student's high school. Again using the Missouri Census Data Center webtool, zip codes were matched to MSAs.

Students were coded as living in an urban area if they resided in one of the 28 MSAs with a population of at least two million people.

Definitions of College-Going Variables

- *Attend any postsecondary institution*: The ELS second-wave student variable F2B07 codes whether a student ever attended any college prior to the 2006 survey.
- *Attend a two-year college*: A student is coded as attending a two-year college if the student has attended at least one postsecondary institution (value of 1 for variable F2IATTND: whether attended this postsecondary institution) that is a two-year college (value of 2 for variable F2ILEVEL: level of institution).
- *Attend a four-year college/university*: A student is coded as attending a four-year college/university if the student has attended at least one postsecondary

institution (value of 1 for variable F2IATTND: whether attended this postsecondary institution) that is a four-year college/university (value of 1 for variable F2ILEVEL: level of institution).

• *Attend a four-year college/university ranked 1–50, 51–100, or outside the top 100 institutions*: The restricted portion of the ELS includes IPEDS codes (F2IIPED) for every attended college or university, which are then matched to tiers of schools in the *US News & World Report's 2014 Best Colleges* list. (Note that by transferring between institutions, it is possible for a student to attended colleges or universities in more than one ranking tier.) It might be argued that the 2004 rankings should be used given that the ELS students graduated in the class of 2004. By the nature of the rankings, very few changes would result from this alternative, and any changes would be at the margins of the rankings. The 2014 rankings, by this argument, create a small degree of measurement error in estimating the college-going of the class of 2004. However, our interest is in choices made by the classes of 2014 and beyond, for which the 2014 rankings are preferable.

Probability Model Coefficients

Supplemental materials available on the book website report, for each of the four family composition types among the native-born and separately for foreign-born, logistic regression coefficients for models of each college-going outcome. Probabilities of college-going are calculated by applying these coefficients to observed demographic characteristics of ACS subjects.

Section 3: Adjustment for Changes in Family Structure

The probability models estimated in section 2 show that family structure correlates strongly with college-going behavior. Unlike most other demographic variables, family structure often changes between the time a child is observed in the ACS and when they are of college-going age. To account for this possibility, the HEDI estimates for each child the probability of living in each of the four family structures at age 18.

As a repeated cross-section, the ACS includes no information about family structure in past years and so cannot be used to estimate the probability of change. By contrast, the longitudinal Panel Study of Income Dynamics (PSID) provides repeated observation of children and their families suitable for this purpose.[7] Using data from the 2005 and 2009 waves, I estimate four-year transition probabilities based on observations of children ages 0 to 13 in 2005. Transformations of these four-year transition estimates yield one-year transition probabilities that are repeatedly self-multiplied to create estimates of the probability of family transition between the age of ACS observation and age 18.

Given that the PSID sample is relatively small, the transition probabilities are conditioned on only one variable. Analysis of variance guides the choice of which variable to include in the model. First, a binary variable notes whether a child's family composition changed between 2005 and 2009. Analysis of variance determines which of the possible exogenous variables contains the most power in predicting changes to family structure: census region, race/ethnicity, family income, mother's education, father's education, and child's age (i.e., all of the predictors in the college-going model except child sex, which seems unlikely to predict family structure changes, and urban status, because the PSID does not contain comparably detailed geographic variables).

Where possible, PSID variable definitions are closely matched with the categories used in the ACS and ELS. However, several simplifications were required due to the modest size of the PSID sample. First, the eight income brackets were collapsed into four by combining categories 1 and 2 and 3 through 6. Similarly, age was collapsed into five groups: ages 1, 2, 3, 4 to 7, and 8 to 13.[8] Also for sample size reasons, census divisions were combined into census regions.

Finally, the PSID does not directly record the child's race/ethnicity. Assignments reflect race/ethnicity of parents, who are matched to children using the PSID's Parent Identification file. The survey records race/ethnicity of the household head and the head's spouse. Heads and spouses who choose any of seven Hispanic descriptors are counted as Hispanics, while all others are considered non-Hispanic. This code is combined with the head's and spouse's race to form the five race/ethnicity groups noted in section 2. When siblings of the head are present in the household, their race/ethnicity is coded to match the head.

With race/ethnicity defined for all heads, spouses of heads, and siblings of heads, PSID children are assigned a race/ethnicity through an iterative process. In a first pass, children's race/ethnicity are derived from the child's mother's and father's race/ethnicity. When the parents both fall in the same race/ethnicity category, the child's categorization is straightforward. When parents are coded differently, the child's category is determined by the following rules:

1. If either parent is Hispanic, the child is Hispanic
2. Except for when one parent is Hispanic, if one parent is of Other race/ethnicity, so is the child
3. If one parent is non-Hispanic white and the second parent is of another group, the child follows the race/ethnicity of the second parent
4. Offspring of Asian American and non-Hispanic black parents are coded as Other.

This first pass based on parent race/ethnicity does not categorize all children in the 2005 PSID, however. For example, if a child is living in a household headed by her grandfather or aunt, her parents' races/ethnicities may be undefined at the start of this procedure. However, the process of assigning race/ethnicity in this first pass may assign race/ethnicity to one or both of her parents. The model iterates on this assignment process until no additional individuals can be assigned a race/ethnicity. This iterative process may still leave children without an assigned race/ethnicity if they live with only one parent (or if only one parent remains in the PSID sample) or if either parent lacks a race/ethnicity categorization at the end of the iterative process. In these cases, child race/ethnicity is defined to follow that of the one parent for whom race/ethnicity is defined.

Having defined all exogenous variables, I apply analysis of variance to explore determinants of undergoing a change in family structure. (Detailed results are available from the author upon request.) The mean squares associated with race/ethnicity, mother's education, family income, and the child's age are 7 to 11 times as large as those for father's education or region. Because many children have missing observations of father's education, the sample can be made approximately one-third larger by excluding this variable from the analysis. Given that father's education is not a significant predictor (either statistically or practically) of composition change in the first analysis of variance, it would appear excluding the variable does little damage to the model while expanding the sample size. After this model simplification and attendant increase in the number of observations, mother's education stands out as the largest determinant of family structure change.[9] (Family income is the nearest alternative variable. Again, results are available upon request.)

Further analysis of the probability of family structure change shows little difference between a mother who holds a four-year degree and one who acquired more education. Given the relatively small sample size of the latter group and the similarity in this probability, the analysis is further simplified by combining these two groups into a single category.

To estimate the probability of transition between family structures, PSID observations are separated by mother's education. Within each group, transition rates between family structures in 2004 and 2009 are noted. Because the 2005 PSID includes no children of a mother holding a four-year degree or more who live with father alone or with neither father nor mother, it is impossible to estimate transition rates for such families. For this particular family structure, the transition rate into other family composition states is set equal to zero.

This process yields a four-by-four family structure transition matrix for each category of mother's education. The next step in the estimation process uses these four-year transition matrices to estimate one-year transition matrices. Let $P4_{em}(i,j)$ denote the probability of moving from family structure i to family structure j over four years given mother's education level e_m. Then

$$P_{e_m}(i,j) = \begin{cases} P4_{e_m}(i,j)^{.25} & \text{if } i=j \\ 1-(1-P4_{e_m}(i,j))^{.25} & \text{if } i \neq j \end{cases}$$

defines the elements of an approximate one-year transition matrix containing probabilities of moving from and to each family structure over a single year.[10] In the final step in the estimation process, one-year transition matrices are repeatedly multiplied to estimate a transition matrix for a child of age a with a mother holding education level e_m: $F(e_m, a) = P_{e_m}^{(18-a)}$. The probability of moving from family type i to type j $F_{i \to j}(e_m, a)$ is the (i,j) element of $F(e_m, a)$.

In addition to the direct effect of family transition on college-going, families transitioning from one family structure to another may experience changes in family income as a second wage earner is gained or lost. To account for this, I note the average change in family income percentile experienced by families moving from one family structure to another as reported in the PSID sample. Because relatively few families move out of single-parent family structures, cell sizes for these family transitions tend to be very small. As a result, estimates of changing family income are limited to transition cells with at least 20 observations; all other income changes are assumed to be zero. Of the 12 possible family structure transitions (excluding cases in which family composition does not change), the following three transitions and associated changes in family income percentiles were noted and used to adjust probabilities of college-going conditional on family composition change:

Family transition	Percentile change in family income distribution
Living with both parents to living with mother only	−11.6
Living with both parents to living with father only	−9.4
Living with mother only to living with neither parent	+28.2

The potential for changes in family structure creates one final challenge when applied to the ACS data: missing parent education. Specifically, when a child is observed living with only one parent, the ACS does not report the education of the absent parent. Because family composition could subsequently change such that the child was living with the other parent or both parents at age 18, the model requires a value for the missing parent's education. Imputation of education for parents not present with the child at the time of ACS observation follows from a regression of father's (mother's) education on years of mother's (father's) education, race/ethnicity dummies, and census division dummies in the subset of data for which both parents are present. A similar method is employed for children living with neither parent. In this case, imputation is based on observed race/ethnicity and census division along with the correlation between these variables and observed parental education.

Section 4: Adjustment for High School Retention

The ELS is designed to be representative of high school sophomores. While most students are compelled to remain in school long enough to be included in the population covered by the survey, older students and those who were held back prior to the tenth grade may drop out prior to the sampling period. To estimate the probability that a child will drop out prior to that time, data from the ACS is used to construct a binary variable for each 16-year-old, noting whether the child is in school at the time of the survey. A logit regression examines the connection between school attendance at age 16 and explanatory variables: sex, race/ethnicity, sex-ethnicity interaction, census division, urbanicity, foreign-born status, mother's education, father's education, and family income. Among children born in the United States, the analysis is performed separately for four family structures: living with both mother and father, living with mother only, living with father only, and living with neither father nor mother.[11] Due to small sample sizes, foreign-born children are analyzed by a single, more limited model including predictors: sex, race/ethnicity, census division, urbanicity, and family income.

Because family structure may change between the point of observation in the ACS and age 16, for each US-born student the probability of dropout is estimated conditional on each of the four family structures. The ultimate probability of leaving school is defined as an average of these retention rates using the probability of transition to each possible family type as weights.

Let $R(s, r, d, i, e_m, e_f, y, f')$ be the estimated probability that a 16-year-old is retained in school given demographic characteristics s, r, d, i, e_m, e_f, y, and family structure f' at age 16. Let $F_{f \to f'}(e_m, a)$ be the probability, given mother's education, that a child observed in a family of composition f at age a lives in a family of composition f' at age 16. Then the estimated probability that a child with demographic characteristics $s, r, d, i, e_m, e_f,$ and y observed at age a in a family with composition type f will be retained in school to tenth grade is

$$R(s,r,d,i,e_m,e_f,y,f) = \Sigma_{f'} F_{f \to f'}(e_m,a) * R(s,r,d,i,e_m,e_f,y',f')$$

Section 5: Adjustment for Migration between States and Metropolitan Areas

The goal of the project is to estimate the number of students attending college by their place of residence at age 18, whereas the ACS headcount takes place at ages 0 to 17. Unfortunately, between these ages, a good number of young people move between states or cities: the ACS reports that 2.2 percent of native-born children ages 1 to 17 were living in a state/metropolitan area different from the one in which they resided one year prior. In addition to noting which children have moved, the ACS also indicates the state and metropolitan area of residence in the prior year. This information forms the basis of adjustments necessitated by migration of native-born children.

The available data present several problems for unbiased estimation of migration rates. First, the ACS question asks about movements from one year to the next. This likely leads to an overestimate of migration for the purposes here. To see why, consider an individual who reports having lived in a different location one year prior. It would not be surprising to observe that individual return to his original location at some point over the next few years. In fact, if the migration data were based on a question of residence five years prior (as the census long form used to do), such an individual would not be coded as moving at all. The goal in the present case is to correct for migration between the age of ACS observation and age 18. This is more akin to the five-year than to the one-year migration variable, but the ACS only includes the latter.

In addition, despite its very large size, the ACS does not include a sufficient number of observations to estimate a model employing all of the demographic variables used by the college-going probability model. Put simply, after dividing the data into $63 \times 63 = 3,969$ pairs of location of origin/current location for each of four family types plus nonnatives, many subgroups have literally too few observations to estimate a model with 33 regressands. The process described next uses the data to guide revision to a more parsimonious model. To summarize the process: First, analysis of variance identifies the demographic variables most associated with migration. Then, observations are divided into a modest number of subgroups according to their attributes in these dimensions. Next, for each subgroup, I estimate a 63-by-63 one-year migration matrix. Finally, the one-year migration matrices are multiplicatively combined to estimate the probabilities of migration from/to each possible location between the time of observation in the ACS survey and the point of college decision making.

Analysis of variance suggests that a small set of variables are stronger than others in predicting migration among those born in the United States: race/ethnicity, mother's education, child's age, and census division.[12] (Detailed results are available from the author upon request.) Of these, the census division is inherently captured in the structure of migration matrices. Similarly, the structure inherently captures any location-specific fixed factors such as the long-term economic strength of the state.

Having restricted attention to race/ethnicity, mother's education, census division, and age, a linear regression model points to ways in which categories within these variables can be combined to reduce the number of estimated transition matrices. Based on these coefficient estimates, I made the following modifications of the variable categories to reduce the dimension of the estimation problem without doing significant damage to the predictive power of the migration model:

Age	group 1: ages 1 to 3
	group 2: ages 4 to 8
	group 3: ages 9 to 17
Race/ethnicity	group 1: non-Hispanic white, non-Hispanic black, and Other
	group 2: Hispanic and Asian
Mother's education	group 1: < HS
	group 2: HS, some college, four-year degree, and > four-year degree

This recoding of the data leaves 12 ($= 3 \times 2 \times 2$) combinations of child's age, mother's education, and race/ethnicity subgroups. For each, I estimate a 63-by-63 one-year migration matrix where element (g,h) equals the observed, person-weighted fraction of subjects who lived in location h at the time of the ACS survey who reported living in location g one year prior. Repeatedly multiplying appropriate one-year migration matrices produces estimates of the probability of moving between any two locations between observation and college-going age. The migration matrix for a child of age a and (modified) race/ethnicity group $\tilde{r}$ with a mother of (modified) education group $\widetilde{em}$, denoted $M_{\tilde{r}\widetilde{ema}}$, is given by

$$M_{\tilde{r}\widetilde{ema}} = A_{\tilde{r}\,em1}^{(3-a)} A_{\tilde{r}\,em2}^{4} A_{\tilde{r}\,em3}^{12} \; for \; a = 0,\ldots,2$$

$$M_{\tilde{r}\widetilde{ema}} = A_{\tilde{r}\,em2}^{(8-a)} A_{\tilde{r}\,em3}^{12} \; for \; a = 3,\ldots,7$$

$$M_{\tilde{r}\widetilde{ema}} = A_{\tilde{r}\,em3}^{(19-a)} for \; a = 8,\ldots,17$$

where $A_{\tilde{r}\,\widetilde{emk}}$ is the estimated one-year migration matrix for a child in (modified) age group $k = 1, 2,$ or 3.

In addition to accounting for movements of children, we must make associated corrections to the probability of college attendance flowing from the change in location. For each college-going outcome, the adjustment incorporates the estimated marginal probability of that outcome associated with census division and urban status. That is, if the probability model estimates that a child with a given demographic profile living in state/metropolitan area g has probability p_g of attending a particular college type, then the adjusted probability of going to that college type conditional on moving to state/metropolitan area h is $\hat{p}_h = p_g + \dfrac{\partial p}{\partial l}_{g \to h}$ where $\dfrac{\partial p}{\partial l}_{g \to h}$ is the estimated marginal change in probability between locations g and h.

Section 6: Adjustment for Mortality

The CDC provides age-specific mortality tables by sex and race/ethnicity (non-Hispanic white, non-Hispanic black, and Hispanic).[13] Assuming age-and-race-specific mortality remains constant over time, mortality rates for each age are combined to create an estimate of the probability a native-born child of age a and race/ethnicity r will survive to college-going age:

$$S(a,r) = (1 - m_{18r})*(1 - m_{17r})* \ldots *(1 - m_{a + 1r})$$

where m_{vr} is the probability a child of race/ethnicity r will die in the vth year of life. Because the CDC does not report separate mortality rates for children of Asian or Other race/ethnicity, I assigned mortality rates of non-Hispanic whites to these groups.

Section 7: Adjustment for Immigration

While the ACS reports the number of foreign-born children of each age by state/metropolitan area, these figures are poor proxies for the number of foreign-born, college-aged children in those localities when these cohorts reach age 18 due to additional immigration, migration between states/metropolitan areas, and (to a much smaller degree) mortality. The combined size of these effects are substantial: the ACS reports more than 10 times as many 17-year-old nonnatives as 0-year-old nonnatives.

These differences were accounted for in the following way. For each age, the number of foreign-born children observed in the ACS is expressed as a fraction of the number observed at age 17.[14] These values are then fit to age, its square, and its cube, imposing the restriction that the regression line must equal 100 percent at age 17. Assuming immigration, foreign-born migration, and mortality patterns among immigrants continue as they have in the recent past, the observed relationship between age and nonnative cohort size can be used to estimate the expected growth for a given age cohort between the point of observation in the ACS and college-going age. For example, if the size of the age-6 foreign-born cohort is estimated to be 33 percent that of the age-17 cohort, then each age-6 foreign-born child in this group corresponds to $0.33^{-1} = 3$ children at college-going age.

Age-cohort size patterns are estimated separately for subgroups of foreign-born children broken down by race/ethnicity and state/metropolitan area. For this purpose, locations were categorized into three tiers of immigration intensity based on the fraction of all foreign-born children residing in the locality. The first group represents two disembarkation points, each containing more than 8.5 percent of the population of foreign-born children in the ACS (the percentage of foreign-born children residing in the locality is noted in parentheses): New York City (11.3 percent) and Los Angeles (8.8 percent). These two cities account for just more than 20 percent of all foreign-born children. The localities in a second tier are each home to more than 2.0 percent of foreign-born children: nonmetropolitan Texas (4.1 percent), the District of Columbia (4.1 percent), San Francisco (3.8 percent), Houston (3.7 percent), Miami (3.7 percent), Chicago (3.3 percent), Dallas (3.2 percent), nonmetropolitan California (2.9 percent), nonmetropolitan Florida (2.9 percent), Boston (2.3 percent), Atlanta (2.1 percent), Seattle (2.1 percent), and Philadelphia (2.0 percent). Collectively, this group contains 40 percent of foreign-born children. The remaining 49 localities form a third tier in which no single location is home to more than 2 percent of foreign-born children. Collectively, this final group accounts for 40 percent of such young people.

Due to the small number of foreign-born children with race/ethnicity codes of non-Hispanic black and other, these two subgroups are combined. For each combination of the three immigration-intensity tiers and four race/ethnicity groups, I fit the cohort size of foreign-born children observed at each age (represented as a fraction of the age-17 cohort size) F on a cubic function of age a. To impose the assumption that cohort size remains unchanged after age 17, the regression restricts the estimate for F at age = 17 to be unity through the no-constant specification:

$$(1 - F) = \beta_1 (a - 17) + \beta_2 (a - 17)^2 + \beta_3 (a - 17)^3 + \varepsilon. \tag{8}$$

Regression (8) is estimated using the sum of observed person weights within age as a weighting variable, thus giving greater influence to larger cohorts. Based on this regression, each nonnative child is assigned a scaling variable S that depends on age, race/ethnicity, and locality:

$$S(a, r, d) = \frac{1}{1 - \widehat{F(a, r, d)}}.$$

Notes

CHAPTER ONE: **Demographic Headwinds for Higher Education**

1. In the classification used by Dumont and Lemaître (2005), North America is defined as Canada and the United States. Countries for which more than 10 percent of foreign-born are from unknown origins were excluded from this analysis.

2. All American Community Survey data cited in this work were accessed from Integrated Public Use Microdata (Ruggles et al. 2010). Geographic regions include the 28 metropolitan areas with total population greater than two million people and 35 nonmetropolitan portions of states. Some nonmetropolitan portions of states are merged to reach a minimum total population of two million people in each resulting area. See chapter 3 for more detail on geographic boundary definitions.

3. "Migration Flows in the U.S.," http://www.pewsocialtrends.org/2008/12/17/u-s -migration-flows/.

4. The total fertility rate is an estimate of the average number of children that would be born to a woman if her fertility rate in each year of her life matched the fertility rate observed across ages in the population as a whole at one point in time.

5. WICHE serves 15 Western states, promoting the sharing of resources among the states' higher education systems. For more than 30 years, they have forecasted numbers of high school graduates.

6. See http://www.people.carleton.edu/~ngrawe/HEDI.htm.

7. WICHE does not report numbers of nonpublic school graduates by race/ethnicity. If we add nonpublic school students to non-Hispanic white public school students, the pattern is nearly identical to that reported here.

CHAPTER TWO: **Demographics as Destiny?**

1. The WICHE forecasts presented in chapter 1 do not ignore this point. Presumably, this concern is one reason the organization forecasts high school graduates rather than population at age 18. Still, the point here remains because college attendance rates vary remarkably by demographic group, even conditional on high school graduation.

2. The relationships in this chapter are bivariate, utilizing no control variables. The model presented in the next chapter incorporates the greater complexity of a multivariate approach.

CHAPTER THREE: **The Higher Education Demand Index**

1. The combined nonmetropolitan portions of states are: Alaska and Hawaii; Colorado and Wyoming; Connecticut, Massachusetts, and Rhode Island; Delaware, Maryland,

Virginia, and West Virginia; Idaho and Montana; Kansas, Nebraska, North Dakota, and South Dakota; Maine, New Hampshire, and Vermont; and Oregon and Washington.

2. It is easy to imagine other subgroups of both two- and four-year institutions. For example, one might be interested in demand for women's colleges or historically black colleges and universities (HBCUs). The nature of the model limits some of these choices. In particular, the category must attract a significant number of the students in the ELS. If, as in the case of women's colleges, only a small number of ELS participants attend institutions in a given category, then the resulting probability estimates will involve so much uncertainty that resulting forecasts are of limited value. In addition, if an institution group does not draw a significant number of ELS students from every demographic subgroup (and the intersection of subgroups), the probability model can't be estimated as specified. For example, HBCUs do not draw sufficient numbers of non-Hispanic whites, Asian Americans, or children from high-income families to estimate the model specified here. Of course, the model could be modified by eliminating variables or altering variable categories. However, differences in model specification then raise questions about comparability across forecasts.

3. Note that attendance at schools in these categories is not mutually exclusive because the same student may attend multiple institutions of different types. Additionally, because *US News* maintains separate lists for colleges and universities, allowing for ties, there are approximately 100 institutions with ranks between 51 and 100, and another 100 institutions given ranks between 1 and 50.

4. The reported distributions utilize ACS person weights.

5. Note that this approach to immigration also captures the effects of mortality and within-country migration within the nonnative population.

6. "Migration Flows in the U.S.," http://www.pewsocialtrends.org/2008/12/17/u-s-migration-flows/.

7. Goldin and Katz take this final estimate from Current Population Survey data.

8. In this and the tests that follow, it bears remembering that the "observed" figures are also estimates that include measurement errors of their own. While this section treats the ACS and NCES figures as "true," measurement errors in these figures will bias the evaluation against the HEDI.

9. An alternative conception of the baseline model could use the populations observed in each location in the 2000 Census scaled up to account for the national immigration rate in the 1990s, a figure that would be known at the time of the 2000 Census. From 1990 to 2000, the number of US residents born between 1983 and 1985 grew by 11.6 percent. After adjusting baseline model estimates for this rate of increase, the result is only slightly better than reported previously. The aggregate error falls to 661,000 (5.2 percent). When the analysis is broken down by location, the sum of absolute errors across locations is essentially the same as reported in the text.

10. The following states were combined to create common geographical boundaries: Colorado and Wyoming; Delaware, Maryland, Virginia, West Virginia, and District of Columbia; Idaho and Montana; Kansas, Nebraska, North Dakota, and South Dakota; Maine, New Hampshire, and Vermont; Massachusetts, Rhode Island, and Connecticut; New York and New Jersey; and Oregon and Washington.

11. While the larger share of Kansas City falls in Missouri, because Illinois's portions of St. Louis were assigned to Missouri, Kansas City was assigned to Kansas to create an offsetting error.

CHAPTER FOUR: Changing Contours of Population and Aggregate Higher Education Demand

1. This is not inconsistent with data on rising undergraduate enrollments presented in chapter 3. Here data are presented on first-time enrollment, whereas the figures in chapter 3 represent total enrollment. The difference is explained by the fact that many people returned to education in the 1980s in response to increasing wage premia.

2. As noted earlier, postsecondary uptake is so high that population and postsecondary demand track each other very closely. Analogous analysis of population would be all but identical, within a percentage point or two for nearly all regions and years. Exceptions are found in the East and West North Central, where projected postsecondary enrollment falls slightly faster than population in the second half of the 2020s, and in the South Atlantic, where anticipated enrollments grow slightly faster than population in the early 2020s. Detailed divisional forecasts of this and other measures of college attainment are available at the book's webpage: http://www.people.carleton.edu/~ngrawe/HEDI.htm.

3. While only 56 percent of these were enrolled full time, this aggregate count corresponds to the "ever-attended" measure of matriculation used in the projections presented previously.

4. This result is fairly robust to altering assumptions on the intensity of part-time faculty work. For example, if part-time faculty are only 0.5 FTE, the number of lost faculty positions falls modestly, to 23,300.

CHAPTER FIVE: Demand for Two-Year Programs

1. These estimates are calculated based on the zip code of the high school and postsecondary institutions attended by each student. Zip codes were converted to latitude and longitude using a database provided at www.boutell.com/zipcodes/. Finally, distance was calculated using the haversine formula.

2. Supplemental materials, including detailed divisional forecasts, are available at the book's webpage: http://www.people.carleton.edu/~ngrawe/HEDI.htm.

3. This trend toward greater similarity across divisions in race/ethnicity and greater variation in parental education remains even after excluding the obvious outliers in the South Central and Middle Atlantic divisions.

CHAPTER SIX: Demand for Four-Year Institutions

1. This estimate is based on the National Center for Education Statistics (2016), table 104.20, as well as population reports from the *Statistical Abstract of the United States* (various years).

2. Because *US News & World Report* has separate lists for national colleges and universities, after accounting for ties there are approximately 100 institutions ranked among the top 50 and 200 institutions ranked among the top 100.

3. These estimates are calculated based on the zip code of the high school and postsecondary institutions attended by each student. Zip codes were converted to latitude and longitude using a database provided at www.boutell.com/zipcodes/. Finally, distance was calculated using the haversine formula.

4. The definitions of these groups speak only to the schools' rankings among national colleges and universities by *US News & World Report*, and have no connection to that publication's distinction between *national* and *regional* institutions.

5. Detailed divisional forecasts for various types of four-year institutions are available with supplemental materials at the book's webpage: http://www.people .carleton.edu/~ngrawe/HEDI.htm.

CHAPTER SEVEN: **Is Anyone Paying for All of This?**

1. Of course, this is not to say that state and federal funding play no part in private institution budgets. Student work, government-guaranteed student loans, Pell grants, education tax credits, and state grants all contribute meaningful sums, even if other sources account for the vast majority of these schools' resources.

2. The subgroup of families with children 18 years old or younger approximates the target market for higher education better than households in general. I report data on household income for comparability with other highly publicized reports. Very similar patterns are present in the families-with-children subsample. (See https://www.census .gov/hhes/www/income/data/historical/families/2013/f01AR.xls.)

3. Negative decadal growth rates are slightly more common at the 40th (1980 to 1984) and 20th percentiles (1982 to 1984), but as shown in chapter 2 children from such households have low college attendance rates, and those who do go to college contribute little to no net tuition income.

4. Some erroneously believe that growth rates in comprehensive fees cannot persistently exceed growth rates in family income. This is not the case because higher education is what economists' term a *luxury good*—a good for which demand increases by more than 1 percent when incomes rise by 1 percent. An example makes the point clear. Consider a family that earns $150,000 and pays $25,000 toward tuition and fees. Suppose inflation-adjusted income rises by 3 percent—or $4,500. Some family expenses such as income taxes, restaurant meals, and retirement contributions are likely to rise along with income. Others such as housing, gasoline, and clothing probably won't change much from when family income stood at $150,000. It seems quite plausible that this family could afford to pay $1,500 to $2,000 more in tuition—an increase of about 7 percent. In sum, income growth is critically important for tuition-dependent institutions, but fees can persistently rise faster than family incomes.

5. Because potential full-pay students represent a small subset of the population, further parsing of the data into census divisions likely results in more noise than signal.

6. See http://www.people.carleton.edu/~ngrawe/HEDI.htm.

CHAPTER EIGHT: **Coping with Change**

1. Identified by Baumol and Bowen (1966), *cost disease* applies to activities in which a fixed amount of labor (or other input) is required. For example, agricultural productivity

has increased by more than 150 percent over the past 70 years. Yet over the same time period, the number of orchestral musicians required to perform Beethoven's Fifth Symphony has remained constant. Productivity gains lead to higher wages for workers employed in those more efficient industries (agriculture in this example). To attract musicians who could pursue alternative careers, orchestras must also pay these higher wages. As a result, the cost of performing Beethoven's Fifth is much higher today than at its debut. Similarly, because the fundamental "technology" of teaching has changed little since the foundation of the University of Bologna in 1088, the cost of a college degree has increased with time.

CHAPTER NINE: **Anticipated Higher Education Attendance**

1. These figures are the author's calculations based on reports of high school dropout rates and college attendance among high school graduates reported in the National Center for Education Statistics' (NCES) *2016 Digest of Education Statistics*, tables 219.75 and 302.20. The levels of attendance reported here are somewhat lower than those reported in chapter 2. This is likely due to the fact that the statistics reported here measure students enrolled in college in October of the year following high school completion, whereas the estimates reported in chapter 2 count attendance at any time in the two years following on-time high school completion. While the level of the estimates for the year 2004 differ by about 10 percentage points, gaps between race/ethnicity and income groups are similar using either metric.

2. Data for Asian Americans were not reported separately until 2003. Attendance rates in this group have exceeded that of non-Hispanic whites by about 10 to 15 percentage points. There is some indication that this gap has increased, though the time span covered by the data is too short to discern a trend.

3. These figures are the author's calculations based on reports of high school dropout rates and college attendance among high school graduates reported in the NCES's *2016 Digest of Education Statistics*, tables 219.75 and 302.30. Estimates are based on the product of rates of high school completion and college enrollment because the NCES only reports college attendance conditional on high school completion. Unfortunately, the NCES reports these rates for different subgroups of the income distribution. For high school completion, low- and high income correspond to the bottom and top income quintiles, while for college enrollment extreme incomes are defined by the highest and lowest quartiles.

4. Author's calculations based on five-year moving averages of data in the General Social Survey, 1972–2014 (Smith et al. 2015).

5. The logic here is identical to that in the often-told joke (among Harvard graduates, presumably) about the Harvard student who transferred to Yale, causing the mean intelligence to rise at both institutions.

CHAPTER TEN: **The Potential for Policy to Affect Attendance Rates**

1. The following were drawn from the official campaign sites of Ben Carson, Hillary Clinton, Ted Cruz, Martin O'Malley, Bernie Sanders, Marco Rubio, and Donald Trump on December 28, 2015.

2. Simplified financial aid applications could also be categorized as an effort to reduce costs. However, such simplification might broaden prospective students' horizons even without any actual reduction in costs if some families lack familiarity with the financial aid process.

3. While quantifying the potential magnitudes of "free college" proposals, this chapter is not intended to endorse these changes. Bowen and McPherson (2016) make strong arguments against such policy on both efficiency and equity grounds. Specifically, they note that time to completion would likely increase were college costless to students, thus wasting years that could be otherwise profitably employed. Moreover, they argue such a system would be unfair, as it would inevitably result in low-income families (who are less likely to benefit from college subsidies) subsidizing high-income families.

4. Of course, states vary in their support of higher education. Interestingly, only New Hampshire appropriates fewer higher education dollars per full-time equivalent student than Senator Sanders's Vermont (SHEEO 2016). Vermont claims first place in requiring students to bear the largest share of higher education costs—84.9 percent compared to an average of 46.5 percent in all other states. As a result, a policy of free community college might produce meaningful enrollment effects in a state like Vermont, which provides such low state support for higher education.

5. The analyses in this section do not break four-year attendance projections into regional, national, and elite institutions because the predicted effects of reducing income and race/ethnicity effects on attendance at national and elite schools are simply too large to be believed. Income and race/ethnicity play such a large role in attendance at these schools that it is impossible to imagine halving these effects in such a short time. For example, if we were to halve income effects, the HEDI predicts one-third more students would attend national and elite colleges. Even if it were possible to mitigate the importance of income to such a degree, it seems unlikely that national and elite colleges would increase their admissions to take on so many new students. And so it seems more reasonable to consider four-year institutions as a group.

6. As in chapter 9, in this analysis high-income families are those whose incomes fall in the top eighth of incomes for families with a child in a given birth cohort. Low income refers to all others.

CHAPTER ELEVEN: **Looking Beyond 2030**

1. See http://www.people.carleton.edu/~ngrawe/HEDI.htm.

APPENDIX: **Methodological Appendix**

1. Migration among those not born in the United States is captured in the adjustment for immigration described in section 7. Thus the migration transition matrix for foreign-born children is the identity matrix.

2. $\Delta P_j (d,d') = 0$ for all nonnative children by definition.

3. As in the case of migration between states and metropolitan areas, the effects of mortality among the foreign-born is accounted for in the adjustments for immigration described in section 7.

4. See http://www.people.carleton.edu/~ngrawe/HEDI.htm.

5. The 2000 Census and 2011 American Community Survey data were obtained from the IPUMS-USA collection (https://usa.ipums.org/usa/): Steven Ruggles, J. Trent Alexander, Katie Genadek, Ronald Goeken, Matthew B. Schroeder, and Matthew Sobek, Integrated Public Use Microdata Series: Version 5.0 [Machine-readable database] (Minneapolis: Minnesota Population Center [producer and distributor], 2010). While IPUMS does offer data from the 2012 and 2013 ACS, at this time neither dataset includes information on a variable crosswalking PUMAs of migration to standard PUMAs. Without this information, it is impossible to make adjustments for migration.

6. http://mcdc2.missouri.edu/websas/geocorr2k.html.

7. Initiated in 1968, the PSID has three subsamples: one nationally representative sample and oversamples of low-income families and nonnatives. The estimates used here are based on the representative subsample.

8. These reductions in categories were guided by the similarity of coefficients in a linear regression model of family composition change including full sets of dummy variables and all of the explanatory variables mentioned in section 2.

9. The results are practically unchanged when the same model is estimated conditional on a nonmissing value for father's education. This makes clear that it is the colinearity between parents' education rather than the sample composition that explains why the power of mother's education changes between the two models. Mother's education is also the variable most associated with family structure change when exogenous variables are examined one by one.

10. This approximation is necessary because not all of the four-year transition matrices are positive semidefinite. It can be easily shown, however, that the approximated one-year transition matrices raised to the fourth power yield results that are very, very close to the observed four-year transition matrices.

11. For each family structure, I include only the education(s) of the parent(s) living with the child.

12. Migration within the country among those not born in the United States is captured in the adjustment for immigration described in section 7.

13. ftp://ftp.cdc.gov/pub/Health_Statistics/NCHS/Publications/NVSR/61_03/.

14. Ideally, we would express cohort size relative to the number of young people at the point of the college-going decision. Unfortunately, 18-year-old children in the ACS include both those making college decisions and those who are one year beyond that point. Because those who have moved beyond the college-going decision may have moved states to follow their post–high school plans, the sample must be limited to those younger than 18. This means the adjustments described here err to the degree that additional immigration and migration occurs between the ages of 17 and 18. However, empirically this error is very small.

References

Abraham, Katharine G., and Melissa A. Clark. 2006. "Financial Aid and Students' College Decisions: Evidence from the District of Columbia Tuition Assistance Grant Program." *Journal of Human Resources* 41 (3): 578–610.

Allgood, Sam, and Arthur Snow. 1998. "The Marginal Cost of Raising Tax Revenue and Redistributing Income." *Journal of Political Economy* 106 (6): 1246–73.

Altbach, Philip G. 2016a. "Harsh Realities: The Professoriate in the Twenty-First Century." In *American Higher Education in the Twenty-First Century*, edited by Michael N. Bastedo, Philip G. Altbach, and Patricia Gumport, 84–109. Baltimore: Johns Hopkins University Press.

———. 2016b. "Patterns of Higher Education Development." In *American Higher Education in the Twenty-First Century*, edited by Michael N. Bastedo, Philip G. Altbach, and Patricia Gumport, 191–211. Baltimore: Johns Hopkins University Press.

Auguste, Byron G., Adam Cota, Kartik Jayaram, and Martha C. Laboissiere. 2010. *Winning by Degrees: The Strategies of Highly Productive Higher-Education Institutions.* New York: McKinsey and Company.

Bahr, Peter Riley, and Jillian Leigh Gross. 2016. "Community Colleges." In *American Higher Education in the Twenty-First Century*, edited by Michael N. Bastedo, Philip G. Altbach, and Patricia Gumport, 462–502. Baltimore: Johns Hopkins University Press.

Ballard, Charles L. 1988. "The Marginal Efficiency Cost of Redistribution." *American Economic Review* 78 (5): 1019-10.

Bartel, Ann P. 1989. "Where Do the New US Immigrants Live?" *Journal of Labor Economics* 7 (4): 371–91.

Baumol, William, and William Bowen. 1966. *Performing Arts—The Economic Dilemma: A Study of Problems Common to Theater, Opera, Music and Dance.* New York: Twentieth Century Fund.

Beaudry, Paul, David A. Green, and Benjamin M. Sand. 2016. "The Great Reversal in the Demand for Skill and Cognitive Tasks." *Journal of Labor Economics* 34 (S1): S199-S247.

Becker, Gary S. 1981. *A Treatise on the Family.* Cambridge, MA: Harvard University Press.

———. 1986. "Human Capital and the Rise and Fall of Families." *Journal of Labor Economics* 4 (3 pt. 2): S1-S39.

Becker, Gary S., and Nigel Tomes. 1979. "An Equilibrium Theory of the Distribution of Income and Intergenerational Mobility." *Journal of Political Economy* 87 (6): 1153–89.

Bernard, Robert M., Eugene Borokhovski, R. F. Schmid, Rana Tamim, and Philip C. Abrami. 2014. "A Meta-Analysis of Blended Learning and Technology Use in Higher

Education: From the General to the Applied." *Journal of Computing in Higher Education* 26 (1): 87–122.

Blumenstyk, Goldie. 2015. *American Higher Education in Crisis? What Everyone Needs to Know*. New York: Oxford University Press.

Bok, Derek. 2013. *Higher Education in America*. Princeton, NJ: Princeton University Press.

Borjas, George J. 1999. "Immigration and Welfare Magnets." *Journal of Labor Economics* 17 (4): 607–37.

Bowen, William G., and Michael S. McPherson. 2016. *Lesson Plan: An Agenda for Change in American Higher Education*. Princeton, NJ: Princeton University Press.

Browning, Edgar K., and William R. Johnson. 1984. "The Trade-Off between Equality and Efficiency." *Journal of Political Economy* 92 (2): 175–203.

Brücker, Herbert, Gil S. Epstein, Barry McCormick, Gilles Saint-Paul, Alessandra Venturini, and Klaus Zimmermann. 2002. "Welfare State Provision." In *Immigration Policy and the Welfare State*, edited by Tito Boeri, Gordon Hanson, and Barry McCormick, 66–90. Oxford: Oxford University Press.

Bureau of Labor Statistics. 2014. "Women in the Labor Force: A Databook." BLS Reports no. 1052, December. http://www.bls.gov/opub/reports/womens-databook/archive/women-in-the-labor-force-a-databook-2014.pdf.

Cameron, Stephen V., and James J. Heckman. 1998. "Life Cycle Schooling and Dynamic Selection Bias: Models and Evidence for Five Cohorts of American Males." *Journal of Political Economy* 106 (2): 262–333.

———. 1999. "Can Tuition Policy Combat Rising Wage Inequality?" In *Financing College Tuition: Government Policies and Educational Priorities*, edited by Marvin Kosters, 76–124. Washington, DC: American Enterprise Institute Press.

———. 2001. "The Dynamics of Educational Attainment for Black, Hispanic, and White Males." *Journal of Political Economy* 109 (3): 455–99.

Card, David. 1999. "The Causal Effect of Education on Earnings." In *Handbook of Labor Economics*, edited by Orley Ashenfelter and David Card, 1801–63. Amsterdam: Elsevier Science/North Holland.

———. 2001. "Estimating the Return to Schooling: Progress on Some Persistent Economic Problems." *Econometrica* 69 (5): 1127–60.

Carneiro, Paul, and James J. Heckman. 2002. "The Evidence on Credit Constraints in Post-Secondary Schooling." *Economic Journal* 112 (482): 989–1018.

———. 2003. "Human Capital Policy." In *Inequality in America*, edited by Benjamin M. Friedman, 77–240. Cambridge, MA: MIT Press.

Carnevale, Anthony P., Nicole Smith, and Jeff Strohl. 2010. *Help Wanted: Projections of Jobs and Education Requirements through 2018*. Washington, DC: Georgetown Center on Education and the Workforce.

Census Bureau. 2012. *Statistical Abstract of the United States*. Washington, DC: US Government Printing Office.

Centers for Disease Control and Prevention. 2015. *National Vital Statistics Reports* 64 (12). https://www.cdc.gov/nchs/data/nvsr/nvsr64/nvsr64_12.pdf

———. 2016. *National Vital Statistics Reports* 66 (1). https://www.cdc.gov/nchs/data/nvsr/nvsr66/nvsr66_01.pdf

Cherlin, Andrew, Erin Cumberworth, S. Philip Morgan, and Christopher Wimer. 2013. "The Effects of the Great Recession on Family Structure and Fertility." *Annals of the American Academy of Political and Social Science* 650 (1): 214–31.

College Board. 2005. *The Impact of Demographic Change on Higher Education: Summary of Conference Discussions, July 27–28, 2005, Philadelphia, Pennsylvania.* http://www.collegeboard.com/prod_downloads/highered/de/ed_summary.pdf

———. 2016. *Trends in College Pricing 2016.* https://trends.collegeboard.org/sites/default/files/2016-trends-college-pricing-web_1.pdf.

Curtis, John W., and Saranna Thornton. 2013. *Here's the News: The Annual Report on the Economic Status of the Profession 2012–13.* American Association of University Professors, March-April. http://www.aaup.org/sites/default/files/files/2013%20Salary%20Survey%20Tables%20and%20Figures/report.pdf.

De Giorgi, Giacomo, and Michele Pellizzari. 2009. "Welfare Migration in Europe." *Labour Economics* 16 (4): 353–63.

DeLong, J. Bradford, Claudia C. Goldin, and Lawrence F. Katz. 2003. "Sustaining US Economic Growth." In *Agenda for the Nation*, edited by Henry Aaron, James Lindsay, and Pietro Nivola, 17–60. Washington, DC: Brooking Institution Press.

DeNavas-Walt, Carmen, and Bernadette D. Proctor. 2014. *Income and Poverty in the United States: 2013.* US Census Bureau Current Population Reports. Washington, DC: United States Census Bureau.

Department of Homeland Security. 2016. *Yearbook of Immigration Statistics: 2015.* Washington, DC: US Government Printing Office.

Desrochers, Donna M., and Rita Kirshstein. 2014. *Labor Intensive or Labor Expensive? Changing Staffing and Compensation Patterns in Higher Education.* Delta Cost Project at American Institutes for Research, February.

Dumont, Jean-Christophe, and Georges Lemaître. 2005. "Counting Immigrants and Expatriates in OECD Counties: A New Perspective." Organisation for Economic Co-operation and Development Social, Employment and Migration Working Papers, no. 25.

Dynarski, Susan. 2000. "Hope for Whom? Financial Aid for the Middle Class and Its Impact on College Attendance." *National Tax Journal* 53 (3): 629–61.

———. 2002. "The Behavioral and Distributional Implications of Aid for College." *American Economic Review* 92 (2): 279–85.

Ellwood, David, and Thomas Kane. 2000. "Who is Getting a College Education? Family Background and the Growing Gaps in Enrollment." In *Securing the Future: Investing in Children from Birth to College*, edited by Sheldon Danziger and Jane Waldfogel, 283–324. New York: Russell Sage.

Fiske, Edward B. 1980. "Enrollment May Not Fall, After All." *New York Times*, December 9, C1.

Goldin, Claudia C., and Lawrence F. Katz. 2006. "The Homecoming of American College Women: The Reversal of the College Gender Gap." *Journal of Economic Perspectives* 20 (4): 133–56.

———. 2008. *The Race between Education and Technology.* Cambridge, MA: Harvard University Press.

Goldstein, Joshua R., Michaela Kreyenfeld, Aiva Jasilioneine, and Deniz Karaman Örsal. 2013. "Fertility Reactions to the 'Great Recession' in Europe: Recent Evidence from Order-Specific Data." *Demographic Research* 29 (4): 85–104.

Grawe, Nathan D. 2004. "Reconsidering the Use of Nonlinearities in Intergenerational Earnings Mobility as a Test for Credit Constraints." *Journal of Human Resources* 39 (3): 813–27.

———. 2007. "Education and Economic Mobility." Pew Charitable Trusts Economic Mobility Project. http://www.urban.org/sites/default/files/alfresco/publication-pdfs/1001157 -Education-and-Economic-Mobility.PDF.

———. 2008. "The Quality-Quantity Trade-Off in Fertility across Parent Earnings Levels: A Test for Credit Market Failure." *Review of Economics of the Household* 6 (1): 29–45.

Grawe, Nathan D., and Casey B. Mulligan. 2002. "Economic Interpretations of Intergenerational Correlations." *Journal of Economic Perspectives* 16 (3): 45–58.

Haveman, Robert, and Timothy Smeeding. 2006. "The Role of Higher Education in Social Mobility." *The Future of the Children* 16 (2): 125–50.

Hoefer, Michael, Nancy Rytina, and Bryan Baker. 2012. *Estimates of the Unauthorized Immigrant Population Residing in the United States: January 2011.* Department of Homeland Security Office of Immigration Statistics Population Estimates, March.

Hoover, Eric. 2013a. "Demographic Change Doesn't Mean the Sky's Falling." *Head Count* blog. *Chronicle of Higher Education.* June 18. http://chronicle.com/blogs/headcount /demographic-change-doesnt-mean-the-skys-falling/35223.

———. 2013b. "Minority Applicants to Colleges Will Rise Significantly by 2020." *Chronicle of Higher Education,* January 10. http://chronicle.com/article/Wave-of-Diverse -College/136603.

Hoxby, Caroline M. 2009. "The Changing Selectivity of American Colleges." *Journal of Economic Perspectives* 23(4): 95–118.

Institute of International Education. 2015. *International Student Enrollment Trends, 1948/49–2014/15.* Open Doors Report on International Educational Exchange.

Johnstone, D. Bruce. 2016. "Financing American Higher Education: Reconciling Institutional Financial Viability and Student Affordability." In *American Higher Education in the Twenty-First Century,* edited by Michael N. Bastedo, Philip G. Altbach, and Patricia Gumport, 310–44. Baltimore: Johns Hopkins University Press.

Kane, Thomas. 1994. "College Entry by Blacks since 1970: The Role of College Costs, Family Background, and the Returns to Education." *Journal of Political Economy* 102 (5): 878–911.

———. 2004. "College-Going and Inequality." In *Social Inequality,* edited by Kathryn M. Neckerman, 319–54. New York: Russell Sage Foundation.

Kennedy, John F. 1959. *A Nation of Immigrants.* New York: Anti-Defamation League.

Kolodny, Annette. 1998. *Failing the Future: A Dean Looks at Higher Education in the Twenty-First Century.* Durham, NC: Duke University Press.

Krueger, Alan B. 2003. "Inequality, Too Much of a Good Thing." In *Inequality in America,* edited by Benjamin M. Friedman, 1–76. Cambridge, MA: MIT Press.

Kumar, Amal, and Michael Hurwitz. 2015. "Supply and Demand in the Higher Education Market: College Enrollment." College Board Research Brief, February.

Lipka, Sara. 2014. "Colleges, Here Is Your Future." *Chronicle of Higher Education*, January 24, A24-A27.

McGee, Jon. 2016. *Breakpoint: The Changing Marketplace for Higher Education*. Baltimore: Johns Hopkins University Press.

McGuinness, Aims C., Jr. 2016. "The States and Higher Education." In *American Higher Education in the Twenty-First Century*, edited by Michael N. Bastedo, Philip G. Altbach, and Patricia Gumport, 238–80. Baltimore: Johns Hopkins University Press.

Means, Barbara, Yukie Toyama, Robert Murphy, Marianne Bakia, and Karla Jones. 2010. *Evaluation of Evidence-Based Practices in Online Learning: A Meta-Analysis and Review of Online Learning Studies*. Washington, DC: US Department of Education Office of Planning, Evaluation, and Policy Development.

Mumper, Michael, Lawrence E. Gladieux, Jacqueline E. King, and Melanie Corrigan. 2016. "The Federal Government in Higher Education." In *American Higher Education in the Twenty-First Century*, edited by Michael N. Bastedo, Philip G. Altbach, and Patricia Gumport, 212–37. Baltimore: Johns Hopkins University Press.

National Association of College and University Business Officers. 2016. *The 2015 NACUBO Tuition Discounting Study*. Washington, DC: National Association of College and University Business Officers.

National Center for Education Statistics. 2013. *Digest of Education Statistics*. Washington, DC: US Department of Education.

———. 2015. *Digest of Education Statistics*. Washington, DC: US Department of Education.

———. 2016. *Digest of Education Statistics*. Washington, DC: US Department of Education.

Neumann, Anna, and Corbin M. Campbell. 2016. "Homing in on Learning and Teaching: Current Approaches and Future Directions for Higher Education Policy." In *American Higher Education in the Twenty-First Century*, edited by Michael N. Bastedo, Philip G. Altbach, and Patricia Gumport, 401–31. Baltimore: Johns Hopkins University Press.

Okun, Arthur M. 1975. *Equality and Efficiency: The Big Tradeoff*. Washington, DC: Brookings Institution.

O'Neil, Robert M. 2016. "Academic Freedom: Past, Present, and Future." In *American Higher Education in the Twenty-First Century*, edited by Michael N. Bastedo, Philip G. Altbach, and Patricia Gumport, 35–59. Baltimore: Johns Hopkins University Press.

Organisation for Economic Co-operation and Development. 2015. *Education at a Glance*. http://www.keepeek.com/Digital-Asset-Management/oecd/education/education-at-a -glance-2015_eag-2015-en#page1.

Perna, Laura W., and Roman Ruiz. 2016. "Technology: The Solution to Higher Education's Pressing Problems?" In *American Higher Education in the Twenty-First Century*, edited by Michael N. Bastedo, Philip G. Altbach, and Patricia Gumport, 432–61. Baltimore: Johns Hopkins University Press.

Radwin, David, Jennifer Wine, Peter Siegel, and Michael Bryan. 2013. *2011–12 National Postsecondary Student Aid Study (NPSAS: 12): Student Financial Aid Estimates for 2011– 12* (NCESW 2013-165). Institute of Education Studies, US Department of Education. Washington, DC: National Center for Education Statistics. https://nces.ed.gov /pubs2013/2013165.pdf.

Razin, Assaf, and Jackline Wahba. 2015. "Welfare Magnet Hypothesis, Fiscal Burden, and Immigration Skill Selectivity." *Scandinavian Journal of Economics* 117 (2): 369–402.

Ruggles, Steven J., Trent Alexander, Katie Genadek, Ronald Goeken, Matthew B. Schroeder, and Matthew Sobek. 2010. *Integrated Public Use Microdata Series: Version 5.0.* Machine-readable database. Minneapolis: Minnesota Population Center.

Schoen, Robert. 2004. "Timing Effects and the Interpretation of Period Fertility." *Demography* 41 (4): 801–19.

Smith, Adam. 1776. *An Inquiry into the Nature and Causes of the Wealth of Nations.* Edited by W. B. Todd. Indianapolis: Liberty Fund, 1981.

Smith, Daryl G. 2016. "The Diversity Imperative: Moving to the Next Generation." In *American Higher Education in the Twenty-First Century,* edited by Michael N. Bastedo, Philip G. Altbach, and Patricia Gumport, 375–400. Baltimore: Johns Hopkins University Press.

Smith, Tom W., Peter Marsden, Michael Hout, and Jibum Kim. 2015. *General Social Surveys, 1972–2014.* Sponsored by the National Science Foundation. Chicago: National Opinion Research Center.

Sobotka, Tomáš, Vegard Skirbekk, and Dimiter Philipov. 2011. "Economic Recession and Fertility in the Developed World." *Population and Development Review* 37 (2): 267–306.

State Higher Education Executive Officers Association. 2016. *State Higher Education Finance: 2015.* http://sheeo.org/sites/default/files/project-files/SHEEO_FY15_Report_051816.pdf.

Stigler, George J. 1958. "The Economies of Scale." *Journal of Law and Economics* 1 (1): 54–71.

Western Interstate Commission for Higher Education. 2016. "Knocking at the College Door: Projections of High School Graduates, December 2016." https://knocking.squarespace.com/s/All-Projections-Published-Table-Format-en76.xlsx.

Index